I0037687

DREAM DRIVEN

THE STEP-BY-STEP PROCESS TO DISCOVER YOUR PERFECT BUSINESS IDEA AND LAUNCH IT THIS YEAR

JASON VANDEVERE

Dream Driven: The step-by-step process to discover your perfect business idea and launch it this year
© Copyright 2025 Jason VanDevere

All rights reserved. No part of this publication may be reproduced, distributed or transmitted in any form or by any means, including photocopying, recording, or other electronic or mechanical methods, without the prior written permission of the publisher, except in the case of brief quotations embodied in critical reviews and certain other noncommercial uses permitted by copyright law.

Although the author and publisher have made every effort to ensure that the information in this book was correct at press time, the author and publisher do not assume and hereby disclaim any liability to any party for any loss, damage, or disruption caused by errors or omissions, whether such errors or omissions result from negligence, accident, or any other cause.

Adherence to all applicable laws and regulations, including international, federal, state and local governing professional licensing, business practices, advertising, and all other aspects of doing business in the US, Canada or any other jurisdiction is the sole responsibility of the reader and consumer.

Neither the author nor the publisher assumes any responsibility or liability whatsoever on behalf of the consumer or reader of this material. Any perceived slight of any individual or organization is purely unintentional.

The resources in this book are provided for informational purposes only and should not be used to replace the specialized training and professional judgment of a health care or mental health care professional.

Neither the author nor the publisher can be held responsible for the use of the information provided within this book. Please always consult a trained professional before making any decision regarding treatment of yourself or others.

For more information, email mail@goalcrazyplanners.com

ISBN: 979-8-9990471-0-6 - Paperback
ISBN: 979-8-9990471-1-3 - Hardcover
ISBN: 979-8-9990471-2-0 - eBook
ISBN: 979-8-9990471-3-7 - Audiobook

DOWNLOAD YOUR ONE-PAGE LAUNCH PLAN

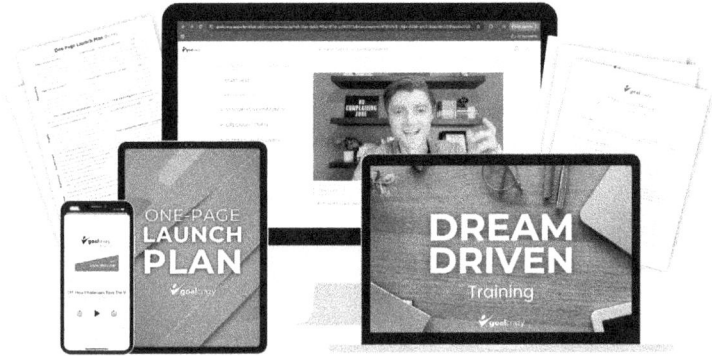

Plus over $100 of additional bonuses FREE!

Access our product design blueprint, goal setting templates, business validation checklist, mindset training, and much more all FREE!

This will help you:

1. Clarify the perfect business idea for yourself
2. Validate your product or service is a winner
3. Get your business launched this year!

People who utilize these resources have been able to get their business up and running faster, so be sure to check them out!

Download FREE at **GoalCrazy.com/freedownloads**

This book is dedicated to my father, for teaching me the value of hard work, encouraging me to dream big, and supporting me in my endeavors.

CONTENTS

INTRODUCTION

How long have you dreamed of entrepreneurship? Is this something you thought of on a whim, or something you have dreamed of for years? If you are like most people I have met, there has probably been a desire in your heart for a while, but for some reason, there has been a hesitation to actually pursue it.

All too often I meet people who genuinely believe having a successful business is somehow off limits for them—like only the other, "smarter" people out there can have it. I used to feel that way! It seemed hard to envision truly having the business I dreamed of.

If you have felt that way too, I want to tell you clearly—entrepreneurship is *not* just for others. It is for you! You are capable of having a successful business, and if you take the actions laid out in this book, you *can* have a successful business. I hope my story and the lessons I share will help you realize that anyone is able to do it.

Look, I am really not *that* smart of a person. There are a lot of other authors out there who are, but I'm not one of them. I am just a normal person who had a dream of being an entrepreneur, and when I was getting my business started I had absolutely no clue what I was doing. I had minimal experience, few skills, and very little money. Yet I have been able to start multiple businesses, generate millions of dollars in sales, and serve tens of thousands of customers all over the world.

Once I started pursuing my dream of entrepreneurship, I quickly realized I had greatly underestimated what a regular person like myself could do.

The same can be true for you! If you have the itch for entrepreneurship, I want you to realize you *can* do it. Even if you have no experience, or no clue what type of business you want to start, the process in this book can work for you. There is a basic method to find the perfect business idea and launch it this year. And not just any business—you can have a thriving business that you *love*. I have realized that even the most complex businesses can be broken down into a handful of steps to start with the right framework.

There isn't a day that passes where I don't think back to the life I had several years ago, when I was working at a job I disliked. Going to work every day drained me. It made me frustrated because I dreamt of entrepreneurship but was afraid to act on it. I lacked direction on where to start. But now, the only feeling I can experience is gratitude. I am so thankful that several years ago I made the decision to push past my fears, pursue my dream business, and create the life I always wanted.

In several years, hopefully, you will look back with the same view! How thankful will you be after you have made your dream business a reality? I want you to know that you can do this. You can achieve your dream of entrepreneurship, and I will do all I can to help.

If you want to become an entrepreneur this year, this is the book for you.

How This Book Works

The book is divided into four parts.

The first part will help you discover and clarify what your dream business is.

The second part will give you the action steps needed to turn that business idea into a winning product or service to sell.

The third part will walk you through how to launch your dream business.

Finally, the fourth part will give you tips for how to grow your business in the future.

Believe it or not, it's a pretty straightforward process! So, if you are ready to get started, flip to the next page and let's dive in.

PART 1

CLARIFY YOUR DREAM BUSINESS

CHAPTER 1

A DREAM DRIVEN BUSINESS

Is starting a business really worth it?

If you already have a well-paying job that supports a comfortable lifestyle, does it actually make sense to walk away from it and start a business of your own? Isn't starting a business risky? What if you fail?

These were many of the questions I had bouncing around my head right before I left my seemingly perfect setup to chase after my dream of entrepreneurship.

You see, in the years leading up to this, I had been working for my family. My dad is a successful car dealer in Akron, Ohio, where I grew up. If you come to Akron, you'll see our last name all over town—VanDevere Kia, VanDevere Cadillac, VanDevere Chevy—you get the idea. My great-grandfather started the business, and I was in line to become part of the fourth generation to own and manage the portfolio of dealerships. All I had to do was work in various departments to learn the business, and after a few years, I would have the opportunity to become an owner.

It was a pretty neat opportunity—one that many people would die for.

However, I was conflicted. After working in the business for several years, I realized I had no passion for it. My whole life, I had dreamed of starting my own business and growing it into a large organization. At first, I thought the dealership would fulfill this dream, because it would give me the opportunity to own, manage, and grow a business. The only thing it didn't provide was the chance for me to actually *start* a business of my own from scratch. But this seemed like such a small detail that I hoped I could push past it, since I had what many would consider to be the golden ticket to success and prosperity.

Even though I had no passion for the car business, I *did* want to own my own business, and the dealership provided an opportunity for that. Wasn't that close enough?

Maybe you can relate to these feelings in your own life. In some ways, you have the career you want, but you still have this desire to do more! Or maybe you have a career you hate, so you desperately want to escape and engage in a business you do love. Either way, you desire the joy and challenges of starting your own business. You want to spend your time building your own company rather than someone else's. You desperately crave the freedom entrepreneurship brings—freedom of time, decisions, income, location, and life. You want a career you are totally passionate about.

When I was working at the dealership, I had two big dreams in my heart. First: To design and publish a planner that would help people accomplish their goals. Second: To invest in real estate and own a portfolio of apartments.

The trouble was, I was terrified to leave my job! Worse, I had no clue how to start either business. These fears lead me to procrastinate. I figured I would wait until "next year" to start, or even wait until retirement when I had more time and money to dedicate toward it.

The longer I procrastinated, the more frustration started to build up. I was frustrated that I was denying the entrepreneurial ideas that I truly wanted to pursue. I started to hate going to my job every day. Even though I was good at the work, it drained me. It left me tired, burnt out, and jealous of other people who were doing exciting things with their lives.

Maybe you can relate to this situation as well? You keep waiting for a "better time" to launch your business. But, the longer you wait, the more frustrated you become with your current situation.

One day, while journaling, I asked myself a question that changed my life: "Do I really want to wait 20 or 30 years, until I retire, to start living the life I want?"

I realized waiting that long would be miserable! Plus, I had this idea for a planner I truly thought could change people's lives. Did I really want all those potential people out there who would benefit from my planner to wait decades to get it, just because I was afraid to take action?

No.

I wanted my planner to inspire others to pursue their ambitions, but if I wasn't willing to take a risk to pursue my own, how could I expect to help others do it? Too often people complained to me that they couldn't achieve success in their life because they didn't come from a wealthy family. I wanted to prove to others that you don't need to have a wealthy family to achieve success—the only thing you need to succeed is the courage to pursue your dreams. So, even though everyone told me it was crazy to leave the family business, in 2018, I did exactly that and turned down the opportunity for ownership in the dealership. I left with a few thousand dollars saved up, a big dream, a ton of fears, and a burning desire in my heart to succeed.

I launched my planner business, Goal Crazy, in 2019, and, although it was challenging, it has exceeded all expectations. It is a business that I truly love, and one that allows the best version of myself to come out and live. I sell planners all over the world, with users in over 12 countries. My business has expanded into coaching programs to help others set and accomplish their crazy goals, and a podcast that allows me to connect with other entrepreneurs. Plus, I have been blessed with the opportunity to buy rental properties and now own and manage a small but growing portfolio of 34 apartments! Most importantly, following my dreams has provided me with the lifestyle and freedom I want for my wife and kids.

I tell you this not because I want to brag about my life, but because I want you to know what is possible. I realize you probably don't have a family dealership, but you do likely have a dream of starting a business, and right now, that dream might seem like a crazy idea. You may have a job that pays the bills, and the idea of venturing out into the unknown seems frightening. That is why I want to give you the framework and confidence to take action and pursue the dream business that's in your heart.

Being an entrepreneur is a completely different way of life. Yes, it has challenges and will push your comfort more than you could ever imagine, but it also allows a deep part of your heart to come out and live. It allows you to live on your own terms, pursuing what you want, with complete control over your time and income. It is fun, fulfilling, inspiring, and purposeful. To me, entrepreneurship is freedom.

Now, I don't want you to just start any random business just for the sake of starting a business, rather I want to help you start a business you *love*. Your dream business. What I love most about my life is having the freedom to spend my time, talent, and energy on things I am passionate about. I have the freedom to set ambitious goals that excite me, and then work hard to create them. Better yet, I get paid to spend my time living my dream. It's incredible!

This is what I want to help you experience. Not everyone is called to start a business, and that is fine. But, if you do find this calling on your heart, I want to help make it happen.

Challenges Of Freedom

Entrepreneurship brings an extremely high level of freedom, which is really good in a lot of ways, but also incredibly challenging. It is hard to have a lot of freedom, and some people don't know how to properly manage it. There is no one telling you what business to start, how to start it, what activities to work on, how much to charge for the work, and no one holding you accountable for following through. Because of this, some people get lost on the journey. I almost did myself. I didn't realize how being an entrepreneur is much more than just a career move. It's ultimately a journey inside yourself.

To help you better understand, let's compare the freedom of entrepreneurship to freedom in an art project. Let's say you are told to complete two art projects. For one, you're instructed to use provided crayons to fill in a coloring book picture of a bumble bee in ten minutes. The next project is to "create a masterpiece you love." That's it—no other instructions. There isn't even a deadline for it. You can spend ten minutes creating a masterpiece, or you can spend ten years creating it.

The second project would be a much tougher assignment *because* of the freedom you have. You have unlimited options to consider. Will you paint something, sculpt something, make a birdhouse, record a song, make a delicious meal, or something else entirely? To decide what you want to create, you need to look inward and clarify what will best represent you and what you enjoy. It becomes a journey of self discovery, how best to utilize your unique abilities to create something beautiful.

This is what a *job* is like compared to *entrepreneurship*. In a job, someone gives you a template of work and the tools needed to complete it, a timeline, and even accountability. A job is like the coloring page.

Entrepreneurship is much more vague, like creating a masterpiece. You have unlimited options, which then trigger never-ending questions, like what business to start, how long it will take, what the first steps are, and what the best strategy is. It can be overwhelming!

Entrepreneurship is so open-ended that for you to succeed, you need to journey inside yourself to better understand what your true desires for life are. You will need to better understand who you are, what excites you, and what strengths you have. You will also need to uncover the fears and limiting beliefs that have held you back from pursuing these dreams in the past.

Now, don't get overwhelmed by this. In the coming chapters, I'm going to give you a framework to clarify your desires, clarify the business you want to start, and clarify the steps to start it. Ultimately, we will uncover a better version of yourself, and the best part, is that entrepreneurship will be the means to let the new you *free*!

The key to making this happen will be choosing the right business idea. Since there are an infinite number of possible business ideas out there this can be a hard decision, so I want to guide you through it step-by-step.

The Two Approaches To Entrepreneurship

The first step in starting a business will be clarifying the *type* of business you want to start. Some of you might already have a pretty clear idea of the business you want to start, while others might not have the slightest clue.

Either way, I want to help.

I want to introduce you to the main two approaches entrepreneurs use when trying to find the perfect business idea. These two approaches are, The Easy Money Approach and the Dream Driven Approach.

Easy Money Approach

The first approach is called the Easy Money approach to entrepreneurship. The Easy Money approach is when you look for a product or service that you can sell with high potential to earn you lots of money quickly and easily. There is no importance as to whether this business is something you are passionate about. You simply view the business as a means to create the income and freedom you want.

At the root of this strategy is the question, "What business will earn me the most money the fastest?"

I have met many entrepreneurs who have found great success with this approach and used it to build beautiful lifestyles. For example, I have a friend, Tim, who found a unique product on Amazon that had very high demand, but abnormally low supply. He had no passion for the product or for running an ecommerce business, but he saw there was a high opportunity to earn money with a very low startup cost. With only a couple thousand dollars and a few weeks of work, Tim launched a business that earned him over $10,000 a month!

The problem with Easy Money is that its long-term chances of success seem to be very low. Since the entrepreneur lacks any passion for the business, if things ever get tough (which is very likely) they give up and search for a newer, easier business. In short, since Easy Money is the foundation of the business, if either the "easy" or the "money" part goes away, the entrepreneur will give up.

Tim had a highly profitable business for almost two years, doing very little work to maintain it. Unfortunately, competition started to increase in his niche. Amazon changed their algorithm and his product was ranked less favorably. Tim never had to work hard in his business before, so he had never learned the necessary skills to run a business in a competitive market. He tried to launch other products, but none of them caught on. The business started requiring a lot of work that Tim didn't enjoy, and the profits were quickly dropping. After a few months of struggling, to my surprise, Tim closed his business and got a corporate job.

I don't write this story to discourage you—I just want you to be aware of the downsides of this approach. Although it is possible to create long-term success with this approach, it is very rare, because there is not enough motivation within the entrepreneur to work through the difficulties that will likely arise. Even if the business works at first, it will create another problem. The entrepreneur's lifestyle will become dependent on the income from the business, and the income from the business will become dependent on the entrepreneur performing work they do not enjoy. Essentially this Easy Money business becomes a new job for the entrepreneur that they don't even like! They then crave an escape from the business and only put in the bare minimum. This makes long-term growth and success very difficult to achieve.

The reality is, starting a business takes a lot of pushing. It requires hard work and effort, and if you have no passion for it, with this approach, you will likely give up before achieving the success you wanted.

Dream Driven Approach

Although the Easy Money approach can work for short-term gains, if you want a sustainable, fulfilling, long-term business, the Dream Driven approach will be a better fit. In this approach the entrepreneur works to discover his or her true dreams and desires for life and creates a business that will fulfill those dreams.

At the root of this strategy is the question, "What do I really want to do with my life?" This approach seeks to answer this question *and* uses a business to fulfill it.

Since the entrepreneur following this method has passion for the business, they will love the work. They will have the motivation and drive to push through the challenging times that are likely to come because the business still gives them the opportunity to live out their dream every day.

Think of the graphic designer who has always dreamed of starting her own studio. Since the business will be connected to her dream, she will be much more willing to push past her comfort zone, go above and beyond for her clients, and work extra hours because it will all still be connected to her dream. Ultimately, a Dream Driven business creates resilience in the entrepreneur to put in the extra work and creativity.

With this approach, the work feels much more like play. Although it will take effort to start the business, it feels light and exciting. The business provides the opportunity for the entrepreneur to better understand themselves, their desires, and purpose in life. Ultimately it allows a deep part of their soul to break free and live! The Easy Money entrepreneur never does this deep work to understand themselves, and then gets confused as to why they are still unhappy, even when they have more money.

A Dream Driven business is what I want to help you create for yourself.

Maybe you are looking to start your very first business, or maybe you currently have an Easy Money business that you want to transform into a Dream Driven business. This process will help.

For some, it is hard to even imagine a business with work that they truly love, that inspires them to act and become a better person. But I want you to know it *is* possible. When you have the framework laid out in this book you will be able to clarify your dreams and use them as the foundation for your new business.

To help discover the Dream Driven business that's right for you, we'll first explore the difference between dreams and goals, and how you can use them to uncover and launch your business idea.

Reflect And Implement

At the end of each chapter there will be an exercise to help you implement the strategies learned. Most of these exercises will encourage you to write out your thoughts.

At first, I hated when books gave me exercises like this—it seemed like extra work.

However, I will tell you that if you don't perform these exercises this book will have way less impact. If you aren't willing to write out your answers, the chances you're willing to actually implement them are far lower.

I want you to make the commitment right now to do each exercise, no matter what. Your dreams are worth it!

I have worked hard to focus the exercises in this book to the core principles you need. None of this is extra fluff. If you want to create the life you desire, commit now to performing the written exercises that are included in the coming chapters.

Are you committed to completing the exercises at the end of each chapter?

- ☐ Yes
- ☐ No

CHAPTER 2

DREAMS VERSUS GOALS

When I was first starting my planner business, I quit my job and spent over six months interviewing successful entrepreneurs. I wanted to learn how they set and accomplished their goals so that I could incorporate their proven strategies into my planner design.

However, during this time, I noticed something unexpected that these successful entrepreneurs had in common. I found that all of them had an ambitious, bold, *crazy* quality to them. I don't mean this in a bad way, I mean it in a great way. Let me explain.

These individuals had *huge* targets, and were crystal clear on what they wanted. They had goals so big that the outside world would perceive them as crazy. But these entrepreneurs went after their desires anyway. They didn't aim for realistic. They aimed for what they wanted—their dreams.

They were also willing to take bold actions, big risks, and get uncomfortable to make their dream business happen. I met someone who bought a motel at the age of only 19. I talked with another individual who convinced friends and family to lend him money to start his business after losing over $100,000 of their money on a prior business idea of his. I met many entrepreneurs who had staked all they had on launching a business they believed in.

These experiences reminded me of the popular Steve Jobs quote, "The people who are crazy enough to think they can change the world are the ones who do." I was experiencing this firsthand!

However, I started to learn there was a method to their madness—they had a system. They had a unique way of breaking their big dreams down into manageable steps that gave them the confidence to take bold actions. This system became the foundation of my Goal Crazy Planner, and is the same approach I will teach you.

I realize that right now the idea of entrepreneurship might feel crazy to you. You probably have many fears and hesitations around pursuing this path. When I decided to leave our family business to go start one of my own, basically everyone told me I was nuts. And, trust me, I agreed! I knew it was a wild idea to start a paper planner business during a digital age. But, once I had the right method to accomplish my dreams, it unlocked unimaginable motivation to make my business successfully happen.

The approach I will teach you will give you the confidence to lean into your ambitious dreams rather than shying away. You will find that crazy dreams will be the most fulfilling to pursue and accomplish.

For this approach to work for you, you must first understand specifically what dreams are and how they connect to your goals.

Dreams

Your dreams reveal the desires of your heart and give you a sense of purpose for your life. When you dream, you are basically asking yourself, "What would I love to do?," and "What would be fun to experience?" Then simply let answers fly out, without any judgment or filters.

You don't have to worry whether they are realistic, or if you know how to achieve them. That's not the point. The point is to let your heart speak to you about what you desire in your life. Dreams are not things you are necessarily committed to achieving. They could be as unrealistic as wanting to own a house in every single state, or as realistic as owning your first home. Both are great dreams.

Dreams are the affinity of all our desires and things we want to do in our life. They are the source of our wants and goals. Dreaming gives us purpose because it allows us to envision something bigger than ourselves, something better than what currently is in our world right now. Dreams come from our heart, they are an innate part of our being.

If you ask yourself, "What is realistic?" versus "What do I dream of doing?", you'll get two very different answers. What feels realistic is often shaped by what you've seen others do before. But asking, "What do I dream of doing?" reveals what you truly want—and that's exactly what we aim to uncover through our dreams.

After you have clarified your dreams, you can look through your catalog of dreams and choose some that you would like to turn into goals. We will do this later in the book. But dreams, in and of themselves, are not goals.

Goals Connected To Dreams

By comparison, goals are simply a tool used to reveal to you *how* to achieve your dreams and lead you into action. Goals are specific targets that you are committed to achieving. They *are* realistic, and you need to have a plan of how to accomplish them. Goals come from the logical parts of our brain and lead us to pursue the things we desire.

Both dreams and goals are incredibly important when you are in business for yourself. There is no one telling you what to do, so you need to have your own sense of direction, motivation, and purpose. Dreams will be that source. Then your goals will provide the means to accomplish those dreams. Look at the picture below to see how this works.

You can see this man has goals that are working toward a dream life, and, more importantly, are forming him into the dream person he aspires to become. Since his goals are aimed at a dream they have purpose which fills him with energy and drive to succeed.

When you start dreaming and connecting your goals to those dreams, it lights a fire inside of you to push yourself and take action. It gives you courage, because you are working to create something you desperately *want* rather than something you *should* do.

This is why you need to have your dreams and goals connected. Unfortunately, our society is not teaching this practice. It only emphasizes goals and disregards dreams.

Goals Without Dreams

Unfortunately, many people have stopped dreaming. They view dreams as mere fantasies or wishes that aren't to be taken seriously, causing them to only focus on goals. The problem with this is that without dreams, you strip your goals of meaning. They become purposeless because your goals won't be working toward a motive larger than themselves. You can set a goal for anything, you can set a goal to write a pop-up book about penguins and then make a plan to do it. However, that goal might not bring you any fulfillment, in which case it would be a complete waste of time. The goal must be connected to a deeper dream. For example, if you always dreamed of studying penguins and writing a book, then perfect! The goal would be in alignment and fulfilling to do. You can turn that dream into a goal and do it!

At the dealership, I was setting all sorts of goals that helped me succeed in the various departments I worked in. However, since my goals weren't connected to my personal dreams they lacked purpose and fulfillment. I was simply working toward a target rather than toward a meaningful dream. This made my actions feel like work rather than play. This led to burnout and tiredness rather than fulfillment and energy.

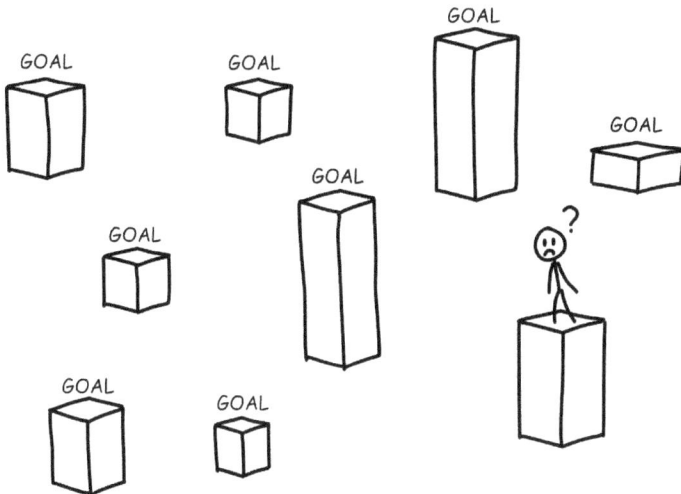

I felt like the man in the diagram above who keeps accomplishing goals, but doesn't feel any sense of direction or satisfaction because the goals aren't leading toward a bigger dream. Unfortunately I meet business owners who feel this way all the time. They stopped dreaming and have disconnected themselves from the source of their inspiration. Now they simply feel like an employee working in their own business to hit meaningless targets.

Over the years of coaching entrepreneurs, I have found that this is one of the biggest problems they have. They simply stop dreaming. If you stop having dreams you stop having meaningful goals. When you stop having meaningful goals, you end up in what I call survival mode.

Survival mode is when you are working hard to simply stay afloat. You lack excitement. Things seem tiring. You are trying to prevent yourself from sinking. You start focusing on everything you "should do" and "need to do" and stop doing what you actually *want*. Obviously, if you stop focusing on what you want, you will never end up with the life you want!

Maybe you can relate with this feeling—like you are working hard toward your goals, but the work lacks purpose, fulfillment and meaning because it is not connected to a bigger dream. Maybe you can relate to the feeling of being in survival mode. If so, dreaming is the key to escape.

Entrepreneurs Are Dreamers

If you want to be an entrepreneur, you *must* be a dreamer. You must be able to envision a future better than what currently is.

Most people agree it is important to dream, but think they are the exception. They think big goals and dreams are only for others, not themselves. Don't fall into this trap!

This lack of dreaming is what I believe to be one of the largest obstacles holding aspiring entrepreneurs back. We are not taught to dream, but rather to push our dreams down and aim for "realistic." Let's be honest— realistic often just means average.

Kids dream all the time, but teachers, parents, or even their peers often shoot their dreams down. This stifles the idea that they have a purpose in this world and leaves them seeking to survive an average life rather than aiming for greatness.

One of the biggest realizations I have had, and have seen others experience, is that we become what we dream about. Our dreams define our life. If we dream about getting drunk with our friends, we will have a life full of drunken late nights. If we dream about starting a business, we will find ourselves pursuing entrepreneurial ventures. If we stop dreaming entirely, then our lives will also reflect that as we end up in survival mode with an average life.

Do you really want to be average? Heck no!

Dreams are what built our society into what it is! Look at all the modern advancements we have—airplanes, cell phones, skyscrapers—these are all a result of people's dreams. Think about the Wright Brothers. If they hadn't dreamt of flying, air travel wouldn't exist. Or Steve Jobs—his dream of making computers accessible to the average person has completely changed our society. Our ability to dream is one of the key characteristics that separate us from animals, without it, we deny our humanity. Our ability to dream is what has led humans out of the wild to build houses, create civilization, travel to new parts of the world, paint beautiful pieces of art, and start successful businesses that serve our society.

What if you truly believed *your* dreams were important? What if you lived your life with the genuine belief that you were born to do something great? What if you believed that you were born to make a difference, to impact our society, and even change the world? What if you believed you were specifically made for a purpose bigger than yourself? You wouldn't just settle for a career that earns a paycheck and then count down the days until retirement. Rather, you would seek a life of impact. You would be excited and grateful to have years ahead of you so you can use your life to serve others and do wonderful things.

Our world needs you to dream and pursue those dreams. There are people who need you to start your business because their lives will be positively impacted by it.

The Process

If you are ready to get started with your own Dream Driven business, here are the steps we will take together: First, we'll work together to uncover the life you've always dreamed of—your ideal lifestyle, the experiences you want to have, and the impact you want to make. Then, we'll map out a business idea that can make those dreams possible. Finally, I'll guide you step-by-step to bring the business to life.

If you are ready to get started, turn to the next chapter and let's start clarifying your dreams.

Reflect And Implement

Ask yourself:

How often do you let yourself dream?

_____

_____

_____

Were you able to relate more with the feeling of "survival mode" or dream driven?

_____

_____

_____

CHAPTER 3

HOW TO DREAM

I always knew I wanted to be an entrepreneur, and, without realizing it, I was given the gift of clarity about the type of business I wanted to start. As a kid, my father would regularly have us create "dream lists." Basically once a year our whole family would sit around the table and make lists of the dreams we had for our life. Some were outrageous dreams, like visiting Mars or owning a private island. Others were more practical, like having a loving family, buying a nice home, starting a business, or investing in real estate.

One of the dreams I regularly had was to design my own planner. I know, it's a weird dream, but I liked planners, and with every one I bought, I dreamt of creating my own. I could also see how having an online business selling planners would provide for the dream lifestyle I wanted for myself and future family. Because of this dream, when I thought seriously about starting my own business, I had a direction for which type of business to start. Any other business besides a planner business would have been a rejection of the true desires I had for my life.

I realize not everyone has this type of clarity. That is why I want to help you uncover your Dream Driven business idea. To do this, we first need to first clarify the dream lifestyle you want your business to create for yourself.

It Start With The Lifestyle

A mistake many people make when they first start clarifying their dreams is only thinking about their dream business. They set up their business as the end destination, and unfortunately, they often succeed. The business completely overtakes their life, leaving them overwhelmcd and stressed. Then, they try and scale back their business to create a healthy work-life balance. This is literally the story of many of my clients that come to me, so don't worry if this describes you. You are not alone!

The key to preventing this is remembering that your business is not, and should not, be the end goal. It is only the means.

Let me explain.

When dreaming about your future, it is important to think about the overall lifestyle you want to have. How much free time would you like, what type of house would you live in, what would your health look like, how much would you be earning, what type of trips would you be going on, what would your faith-life look like, etc. Have dreams for all areas of life!

Once you have a clear vision of the type of lifestyle you want, then you can design a business to be the means to create it.

Additionally, think about how you want to serve others. What type of impact do you want your business to make? What challenges are other people struggling that you want your business to help them overcome? How will your business allow you to be generous to others?

Finally, think about the type of person you want to become. Who do you want to be in the future? What type of characteristics and traits do you want to have? How do you want to carry yourself through life?

After you clarify all this, it will be easier to identify the business that can be the vehicle to create it. Your lifestyle will be the target, and your business the means.

At the end of this chapter, I will provide you with a thorough list of questions to help you clarify and write out the dreams you have for your life. However, I need to first teach you the proper way to dream so that the dreams you create will correctly guide you to a Dream Driven business.

To do this, I will teach you our WILD Dreaming process.

WILD Dreams

When I think of something wild, I think of something without restraints, unleashed, and free.

I want to encourage you to dream in a similar manner. I want you to have crazy, wild, huge dreams for all areas of life. At this point in the process, you do not need to worry about how you will accomplish any of your dreams. Remember, these are just dreams, things you may or may not actually do with your life. We just want to start forming the connection with your heart so you can understand the desires it has.

WILD Dreams have four components:

- **W**inning
- **I**ntegrity-based
- **L**oving
- **D**aring

Winning

Do you think there is a difference between winning and not losing? Think about it for a minute. What is the difference?

If you passed me in the hall and asked how the game went last night and I responded, "We did not lose," would that be exciting news to hear?

Compare that to if I focused on winning. What if I responded, "We won!" That would sound much more exciting, right?

So, what's the difference?

Even though "not losing" and "winning" produce the same outcome, the difference is the focus. Winning focuses on creating an exciting, desirable result, while "not losing" is focused on avoiding failure. I want you to understand this because it is really important to keep "winning" the focus in mind when you are creating your dreams.

Unfortunately, I often see people set "not losing dreams." Basically, they will look around their life and find an area where they feel like they are losing, then they dream about not being a loser in that area anymore. The problem with this is that the dream itself is a reminder they are currently losing in that area of life! Essentially they are creating a dream of not being a loser. Admit it. That's not very motivating. These "not losing dreams" result in very little inspiration to make any real changes.

A better approach when dreaming is to always aim at winning. Simply ask yourself, what would it look like to win? Use the answer to that question to form your dreams and goals. That is what will give you an exciting target and make you willing to make large changes in your life.

Here is an example of this in action. A new client of mine told me his goal was to do $250,000 in revenue in the coming year. I asked him how and why he chose that number. He told me that, the past couple years, he did just under $200,000 in revenue and felt like to be a "real business owner" he needed to be doing at least $250,000 in revenue.

I immediately recognized this as a "not losing goal." He felt like he was losing as a business owner because his business did less than $250,000 in revenue, so he set a goal to not be a loser anymore.

I asked, "What would it look like to win this year?"

Without any hesitation he said, "$1,000,000 in sales." Now, that was a goal I could immediately see lit a fire in him and gave him a ton of excitement. We raised his goal to $1,000,000 in sales and he ended up hitting it by October! When he started aiming at $1,000,000, he acted differently and was willing to make large shifts in how he ran his business.

Compare that to the past few years of aiming at $250,000, where he never made any real changes because he basically had the goal of "not being a loser any more," which killed all his motivation.

Avoid making this same mistake. As you are dreaming, make sure you are creating "winning" dreams.

Integrity-Based

When you are setting goals make sure these goals are sincerely yours and not based on the opinions of others. One of the dreams I commonly wrote down when I was first out of college was to own a helicopter. The funny thing is that I didn't actually dream about flying it, but rather of being able to show it off to other people.

See, after graduating college I had a big desire to try and prove myself and my abilities in the workplace, and for some reason I felt like owning a helicopter would show I was important and therefore worthy of respect. I dreamed about this for several years until I finally realized that I actually had no interest in flying a helicopter at all. The only reason I was dreaming about it was because I thought it would prove I was enough to others, but that is a ridiculous reason to pursue a dream. I realized this was *not* a true, integrity-based dream of mine.

This was eye opening. I then grabbed my dream list and looked to see if there were other dreams I had on the list I didn't actually want. For each dream I asked myself, "Do I really want this? Or is this something I am using to prove a point to others?"

With this in mind, I was able to remove about one-third of the items from my dream list. I was amazed!

I called these false dreams.

False dreams are dreams we don't actually want but use as a means to prove something to others. The sad thing about false dreams is that they are based on the belief that we are currently not enough. We tell ourselves that we are not enough until we accomplish the false dream.

False dreams will distract and derail us from accomplishing our true heart's desires. They are often dreams that purely seek to feed our ego. Although these may seem like they will be satisfying, they will always leave us with the feeling that we need to still accomplish more.

That is why the integrity-based component of this process is so important. It helps us avoid these false dreams by clarifying whether dreams are truly ours or if they are based on the opinions of others. The last thing we want is for you to define your life by other people's dreams. It is hard enough to create your own dreams, don't make it any harder on yourself by trying to also live up to the perceived expectations of others as well!

Now, there is another variation of this mistake I also see people fall into. They dream about doing things people have told them they "should" do.

The psychologist Albert Ellis says, "Stop *shoulding* on yourself."

When I hear someone say they "should" do something, it is an indication that it's not really their desire, but the desire of someone else's. Typically we feel like we "should" do something that others have told us to do. Remember, plenty of people told me I "should" go into that car business.

I want to make sure all of your dreams are truly things you *want* to do, rather than dreams you feel you *should* be doing. You need to remove the "shoulds" and find the "wants." When you follow through on something you "should do" you live up to an expectation of someone else. But when you do what you *want* it lights the fire inside your soul.

After I started Goal Crazy, I had people telling me I "should" write blog posts, post on Instagram, start a YouTube channel, record a podcast, make TikToks—the list went on and on! Everyone told me things I "should" do. And it wasn't bad advice! People have become successful with all of those strategies. But, if I did all the things people told me I "should do," I would drive myself mad! I couldn't do it all.

So, rather than attempting to do all the things I "should" do, I asked myself: Which do I *want* to do? I realized people had been successful doing all sorts of different marketing strategies, and the main factor was finding one they enjoyed where they could be their authentic self and commit to it.

I enjoy writing email newsletters and recording my podcast, so that is what I did. I chose the marketing method I *wanted* to use rather than all the ways others told me I *should.*

The same is true for you! There are an infinite number of paths to success. Rather than seeking what others think you *should* do, ask yourself what you *want* to do. Additionally as you are dreaming, avoid writing dreams that have the pure intention of proving a point to others. You only want integrity-based dreams that are truly yours.

Loving

After I got my first rental property, I dreamed of getting more. I set a goal to have 30 apartments by age 30. For years I had been writing this goal down and dreaming about it, and in February of 2023 it finally happened! I closed on a property which brought my total number of apartments to 34 units. I was only 28 years old. I was excited!

As ironic as it sounds, after I closed on that deal, I lost a lot of motivation. I felt slightly depressed and was confused about why.

I remember when I originally wrote down the dream of owning 30 apartments, I thought to myself, "When I accomplish this, I will be completely happy. I will have total peace and will take breaks in the middle of the day to go on walks and enjoy life."

Now, trust me, I love my life—it's great! But, I cannot say I am filled with infinite happiness and peace.

When I realized I had accomplished my big dream and still wasn't infinitely happy, it took away my motivation. I started to question, "What is the point of working so hard to accomplish my dreams if it isn't going to make me happier?"

I was stuck on this for several months. I lost a lot of drive to try and push toward the next level because I didn't see the point. I figured, *even if I grow my business, it won't necessarily make me happier, so why bother?*

It was during that time I went on a life-changing, six day long silent retreat to reflect. During that time, I realized that for the past several years the way I had been dreaming about my life was completely wrong.

You see, in the past when I would dream, I would *only* think about myself. I would ask myself questions like:

- What do I want to accomplish?
- How do I want to make my life better?
- What habits do I want to start?

Now, these questions aren't bad questions. In fact, I encourage you to ask them of yourself. It's just that I realized there was another set of questions that I was completely missing. I realized I needed to be asking myself questions like:

- What do I want to help *others* accomplish?
- How can I make *others'* lives better?
- What habits do I want to help *others* start?

It turns out the goals and dreams I set for myself using these questions are *way* more fulfilling to work toward. Thinking about myself all the time was a never-ending pit that left me feeling unfulfilled. However, helping others lit me up. I love to see others accomplish their dreams and do things they never thought possible.

When I started to shift my attention to helping others, my business ended up doing better too! Suddenly my eyes were opened to all the unmet needs my customers had. I thought of new programs and courses I could launch to help them reach their goals. When I helped more people, I ultimately succeeded more.

It was during this time I also realized the most valuable skill in the world—your ability to love well. It's the most valuable skill you can have in *any* area of life, and the most desirable skill that others are looking for within you.

It will improve your marriage and family life. That is pretty straightforward. But even in business too, if you act out of a place of love toward your employees, they will be more loyal. If every customer feels that you are acting from a place of love and service, they will come back to you because the deepest desire we all have is to be loved.

If you can get better at loving, you can provide the most valuable gift that all other people are looking for. When you help other people, you receive happiness, fulfillment, peace, and love in return. At the end of the day, that is ultimately what our dreams are working to develop.

I bring this up because I want you to have loving dreams. If all you do is focus on yourself, it will leave you feeling empty.

To be clear, it's not a bad thing to dream about having a nice house or fancy things that you want. I just *also* want you to dream about how you are going to serve others. Most likely it will be your service to others that will be funding all those fancy things you want anyways! I have found it is your service to others that brings more fulfillment than the fancy things do.

We live in a society where success comes from providing a service to others. Just think, where has every dollar you have ever received come from? It has come from someone else. The only way you get money is if someone loves you enough to give it to you as a gift, or if they love the service or product you provide enough to pay you for it. Either way, it always comes from someone else. You are rewarded for how well you love others, not just monetarily, but also with your life satisfaction.

If you learn to act from a place of love, you will have more fulfillment, and you will help make this world a better place. These dreams will lead you to *doing* more with your life rather than just seeking to *have* more.

Ask yourself, "How would I *love* to help others? What challenges do other people have that I would love to help them with?"

It is fun to dream about the things you want to *have*, but it is much more important to dream about the things you want to *do*. Our society unfortunately reverses this. Whenever you share a dream of something you want to *do*, you are often pushed down and told to be more realistic. But paradoxically, the market is always trying to get you to dream of what to *have* next. They want you to dream about *having* a bigger car, fancier clothes, grander vacations, etc. But they don't want to encourage you to desire *doing* more.

Unfortunately, if all you dream about is *having* more things, you likely will not, because having more is going to come as a byproduct of *doing* more. When you *do* more, you will impact more people's lives, which will give you the freedom to actually go have more. If you reverse this, you will become stuck, like many who dream of having nice things, but have little motivation to do the work necessary to actually earn them.

As you are dreaming, ask yourself, "Are these dreams only about serving myself, or will these benefit others too?" Loving dreams do more than just serve yourself. They serve others! Loving dreams benefit your family, community, society and the world.

Daring

I remember when I went to my very first real estate conference. At the time, I owned eight apartments and was 25-years-old, with a goal of owning 30 apartments by the age of 30. I thought I was crushing it!

I was sat down by another young man who looked about my age. He asked me how my real estate investing had been going, and I proudly shared with him how I owned eight apartments. I then asked him in return about his real estate investing. He humbly shared with me how he had over 300 apartments. I was blown away. I later found out he was only 27-years-old and wanted to get to 1000 apartments by the age of 30.

My big ego was immediately shot down and I was humbled to be able to learn from him.

I learned a surprising lesson. I realized that many of these larger investors weren't actually working harder than me. In some ways, they didn't necessarily seem smarter than me either. They were just normal people. The big difference was that they had bigger targets than I did. I had small targets, so I was using small strategies. They had large targets, so they used large strategies.

On the way to the conference, I listened to a book about how to budget my money so I could save up more to invest (small strategy). In comparison, the gentleman I sat with read a book on how to raise money from investors so that he would have the funds to go buy large apartment communities (big strategy).

The interesting thing I learned was that, although the strategies might look very different, the amount of work was about the same. One strategy, however, would push my comfort zone way more than the other.

Looking back, I now know I was aiming too small. Because I had a small target, it wasn't worth it for me to push my comfort zone as much to achieve it. To me, the idea of raising funds from investors seemed scary. However, if I had a larger target in mind, such as buying 1000 apartments for myself, I would have a lot more motivation to take the risk because the payoff of owning 1000 apartments is much higher than owning 30.

I bring this up because I want to show you the power of the target at which you aim. If you aim high, you will have much more motivation to find big strategies and take action on them. If you aim low, you will have less motivation and will therefore utilize small strategies that don't require as much motivation.

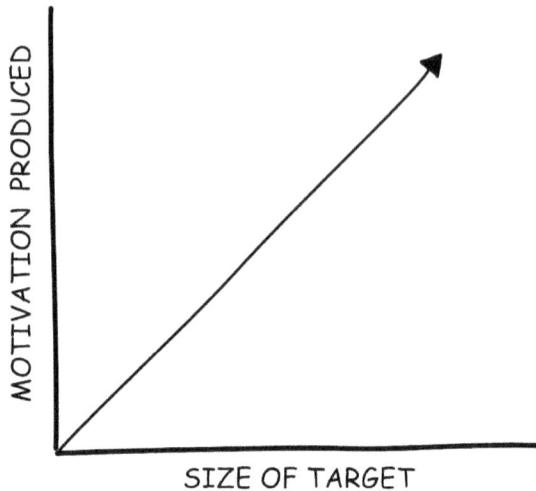

Now, during this phase of the dreaming process you do not need to worry about *how* to accomplish your dreams. Remember, these are dreams, not goals. They are things you may or may not actually do. Later in the book, I will teach you how to use these dreams to form goals and accomplish them.

While you are still in this dreaming phase, don't focus on whether your dreams are *realistic*, rather focus on if they are *motivating*. You need *big*, daring dreams that are enticing enough that you are willing to take bold actions to achieve them.

How To Create Your Dream List

As you write your dreams out, make them specific and clear. Don't just write a vague dream like "traveling." Write down, "Traveling to Hawaii and hiking to the top of a volcano." Make it specific and let your mind experience it. Close your eyes and see yourself traveling to Hawaii, hiking a volcano with a tent on your back, and seeing the lava on one side and the blue ocean on the other. Hear the sounds of the water crashing on the rocks and smell the saltwater in the air.

Think about the details of your dreams. How would it feel to experience them? What would you see? What would you smell? Who would you be with? You don't have to write out each detail, but let your imagination create the experience in your mind's eye. Then, write out a specific dream to capture that vision.

Don't judge these dreams as they come up. There are no bad dreams! Think of how much J. K. Rowling must have daydreamed about wizards before writing Harry Potter. Or how much time the Wright Brothers dreamed about flying before they invented the airplane.

Let your heart reveal the deep desires you have for your life.

Here are some examples of dreams:

- Start a business that earns over $500,000 per year
- Go to Australia for two months and visit each of the five capital cities
- Be a person who avoids all gossip and never speaks badly of anyone else
- Write a book that sells over one million copies
- Climb Mount Kilimanjaro
- Own a home that sits on over ten acres of land
- Participate in a triathlon
- Sail on an Alaskan cruise and see the northern lights
- Travel into space
- Go on a mission trip to Uganda

Dreaming Is A Muscle

When you first start dreaming, it might make you feel uncomfortable or even anxious. It might seem difficult. It is like working a new muscle. It will be hard at first, but will get easier with time, and will even become fun.

You have likely not allowed your mind to think this way in the past. It is very rare that we allow our minds to dream without limits. We almost always limit our thoughts to only what we think we are capable of. By limiting our thoughts, we limit ourselves, because we won't pursue something we don't feel worthy of even dreaming about.

I am giving you permission to dream, to truly ask yourself what you really want to do with your life. Not just because it is fun, but because it is a high payoff activity. This activity alone can bring enough clarity to change the trajectory of your future.

If I never dreamed, I would be unhappy at a job and not know why. If I had never dreamed of starting a business, designing a planner, buying real estate, launching a podcast, writing a book, or coaching people, none of this would exist. All I have in my life I can attribute to taking time to dream about my future.

It's Not Your Fault

Sometimes, when I am teaching people this, they tell me they wish they had started doing it years ago, and spiral into this fear that they are behind in life because they are just learning it now. I want you to know that you are not behind. It is okay if you are just starting this now because your life will change quickly once you start. All the lessons you have learned in the past will be helpful for making your dreams happen sooner.

As a kid, people probably told you to "be realistic," "keep your head out of the clouds," "play it safe," and to "stop day-dreaming." They said this with the best intentions—they wanted to keep you safe and help you avoid struggles. But now you are realizing that playing it safe doesn't lead you to the thrilling life you have been wanting. You need to start allowing yourself to dream and start exploring the great opportunities life has to offer.

Reflect And Implement

Let's put this into action. Get out a pen and paper and make a list of *at least* 50 dreams. This is the rest of your life we're talking about! I am sure you can think of at least 50 things you would love to do, experience, have, or become. If you really want to challenge yourself, make a list of 100!

There is a list of questions below to help you think.

- What type of lifestyle would you like?
- What would you like to achieve?
- What do you want to experience or see?
- Where would you like to travel to?
- What kind of family do you want?
- What hobbies do you want to have?
- Who do you want to become?
- What do you want to be recognized for?
- What do you want to learn?
- What would you like to own?
- What are your business dreams?
- How do you want to help others?
- How much money do you want?
- What are your fitness dreams?
- What kind of home would you like?
- Who would you want to share these experiences with?
- What would you like to provide for your family and parents?
- How do you want to give back to others?
- How do you want to grow spiritually?

For additional help, access our free Dream List PDF and training video at **GoalCrazy.com/freedownloads** or scan the QR code below:

My Dream List

1. _____   26. _____
2. _____   27. _____
3. _____   28. _____
4. _____   29. _____
5. _____   30. _____
6. _____   31. _____
7. _____   32. _____
8. _____   33. _____
9. _____   34. _____
10. _____   35. _____
11. _____   36. _____
12. _____   37. _____
13. _____   38. _____
14. _____   39. _____
15. _____   40. _____
16. _____   41. _____
17. _____   42. _____
18. _____   43. _____
19. _____   44. _____
20. _____   45. _____
21. _____   46. _____
22. _____   47. _____
23. _____   48. _____
24. _____   49. _____
25. _____   50. _____

CHAPTER 4

CHOOSE YOUR DREAM BUSINESS

Do you remember those rom-com movies from the early 2000s where the guy would do ridiculous things to win over the girl, and there would always be some cheesy line in the film like "love makes men do crazy things." As strange as it may sound, when I was working on starting my business, I felt exactly like that. However, I wasn't pursuing a girl. I had a dream I loved and I was pursuing it with everything I had, even if it required me to take crazy action.

I was willing to get up at five a.m. to work 16 hour days, cold call businesses in my industry and ask for help, and get rejected by hundreds of influencers who I begged to feature my planner on their channel. I was even willing to wire all of my hard-earned savings to a supplier in China and risk getting scammed out of the money! I spent over two years working countless hours on my business and only paying myself the bare minimum I needed to survive. It was hard!

The only reason I was willing to make these big changes was because I could directly see how this business would provide for the lifestyle and business that I had always dreamed of.

This is what I want to help you do. I want to help you find the business venture that will make your dreams possible and light a fire of motivation inside of you. I want to find a business that you are so passionate about that you are willing to take bold actions to create it.

Luckily, I have gotten much better at starting new business ventures, so, hopefully, you can avoid spending years in a state of struggle to get yours turning consistent profits. However, I can guarantee that starting a business will challenge you and push your comfort zone, so finding an idea you value is important. Your inner desire should be greater than any of the challenges that come your way. Let's clarify this dream business idea together!

Make A List

Now that you have a list of your dreams for the future, it's time to list out business ideas that could make this dream lifestyle possible. I want you to make a list of *all* the potential business ideas you have. Make a list of at least 20, even if you feel like you already have a basic idea of what you want to do.

These ideas do not need to be fully formulated yet. Maybe you have a desire to launch a podcast but have no idea how to turn it into a revenue-producing business yet—that's okay! Write it down. Or maybe you have giant ideas that you have no clue how to accomplish, like starting your own airline. Write it down! List all the ideas, whether they are realistic or not.

The incredible thing about entrepreneurship is that it is extremely flexible. I have met entrepreneurs who have started successful businesses in the most random industries, and you can listen to their stories on my podcast. I spoke with a successful entrepreneur who sells music that can make leaders more productive or another entrepreneur who sells ice cubes that melt slower than normal.

I had one guy on my show who has a successful business helping people literally do nothing! Well, technically he helps them meditate. I have had the opportunity to meet entrepreneurs who have the most unique business ideas, but have worked hard to grow them into a six-, seven-, or even eight-figure business. Even if your business idea seems random, write it down. I turned my obsession with planners into a product that's generated over a million dollars. Anything's possible!

If your business seems completely generic, that is also okay! Obviously, there are not any truly "generic" businesses, but sometimes it may feel that way. Maybe you want to start a restaurant, a landscaping business, or a blog, and are worried that your idea is not unique enough. That is fine—add it to the list. Finding a business idea that lights a fire in you is the main goal.

Below are some questions that will help you clarify these business ideas for yourself. Use them to list out at least 20 business ideas:

- What would be your dream business?
- What type of business have you always dreamed of having?
- If you already had tons of money, what business would you start just for fun?
- What would be a fun way to use your talents?
- What are the challenges you see others having that you would enjoy helping them overcome?
- What skills come naturally to you that others struggle with?
- What have you learned that others can benefit from?
- What service is lacking in your community that you could provide?
- What would be a fun way to earn money?
- What careers have you seen others have that you thought looked enjoyable?

Really take time to dig deep and answer these questions. If you need to, take a couple days to reflect and research business ideas. Sometimes the best ideas are the first ones, but more commonly the best ideas come later on the list as you start looking deeper into yourself.

The Three L's To Identify Your Dream Business

Once you have your entire list put together, we need to identify which one of your dreams you want to pursue first. This might seem like an overwhelming process, so I will guide you through a few steps to help make this decision more clear. We will use The Three L's to help you clarify which dream business is best to pursue.

The Three L's are: Longing, Lifting and Light.

The right business idea will have all three of these qualities.

Longing

The first step is identifying whether there's a deep longing in your heart to make this business happen. As I have mentioned earlier in the book, you will likely face challenges while starting your business and you need to have longing if you want to persist through those challenges.

There is an easy way to see if there is enough longing in you to make each business idea happen. We will use The First Alarm Test.

First Alarm Test

The First Alarm Test is simple. Are you willing to wake up on your first alarm to make your business happen? If yes, then you pass! If not, then you likely do not have enough desire behind the business idea to launch it.

If a client of mine tells me they want to start a business because they can increase their income by ten percent, I tell them that is not enough. If you earned $100,000 last year and now you want to earn $110,000, I doubt that extra $10,000 is worth making big changes for. That may not be enough incentive to get up on your first alarm and push through all the challenges of the day.

However, if you earned $100,000 and now your dream business has the potential to earn you $250,000, that will be motivating enough for you to push your comfort zone. Earning an extra $150,000 per year is enticing enough to justify making *huge* changes for, including getting out of bed when your first alarm goes off.

You want a longing for this business that is motivating enough for you to get up early, start reading books, seek out mentors, face your fears, and push through your comfort zone to get it started.

The point of this step is *not* to focus solely on the income potential of the business. Maybe your business would let you cut your work hours by seventy percent or finally do something that excites you every day. That can be just as powerful! The key is to determine how much desire is in your heart to make the dream business happen.

Ask yourself, "How big is the fire inside of me to make this dream happen? How badly do I want it?"

Starting a business can be challenging, so you will need a *big* fire inside of you to make it happen. Even the most challenging of businesses can be grown into a success as long as you have enough desire. But, if the challenge is greater than the amount of desire you have, then you will likely give up once it starts to get difficult.

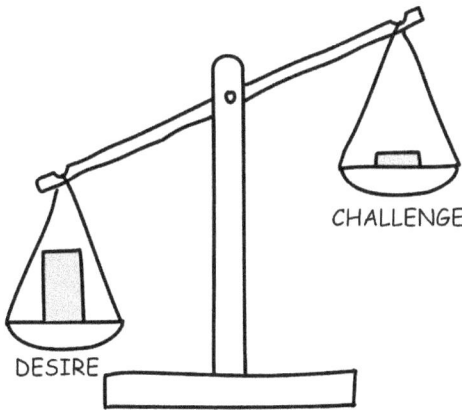

CHALLENGE

DESIRE

DESIRE > CHALLENGE

The only reason I was motivated enough to leave my family's business and spend over two years living on noodles and peanut butter was because I had a burning desire to build my dream business. The desire outweighed the challenges.

Go through your list and ask yourself if you are willing to get up on your first alarm to make it happen. If the answer is yes, then put an "L" beside it to represent the longing. If the answer is "Heck *no,* I am not willing to get up on my first alarm for this," then put an "H" beside it.

Lifting

Next, I want you to go through your list and identify if a business dream is "lifting."

The idea of lifting is that it "lifts" you to the next level. It forces you to improve and stretches you outside your comfort zone to become a better version of yourself.

I think of lifting like surfing.

One summer during college, a few cousins and I moved to Nantucket Island. While I was there I learned to surf. If you have ever surfed, you know that much of your time is spent waiting for the perfect wave. There are a lot of little waves close to the shore that you could ride, but you don't ride those. You swim out deep and wait for the *big* wave, because you know that the big wave is what brings out the best in you. It is the big wave that peaks your performance and stretches you to become better. Even though the big wave is the most risky, it is also the most exciting!

If all I did was ride the little waves, it would hold me back from growth, keep me trapped in my comfort zone, and prevent me from elevating my abilities.

The big waves though allowed me to lift myself to a higher level. Your business should be the same way! It should require your peak abilities and lift you up to become a better person.

One of my favorite speakers, Tony Robbins, talks about how "It's not about the goal, it's about becoming the person who can achieve the goal." This business should force you to improve. It should cause a better version of yourself to break free, just like the big wave.

A "lifting" business is one that is too big for you to achieve right now.

That's right! It is so big that it is outside of your current abilities. Therefore the *only* way you can start this business is if you force yourself to grow your capacity. The point of your dream business is to help you break through your current level and lift you to where you want to be.

Whenever I start a new business, I ask myself:

- What new skills will I need to learn in order to accomplish this?
- What are ways I will need to improve?
- What fears will I need to overcome?
- What limiting beliefs will I need to work through?

This helps me not only accomplish the goals I want, but, more importantly, become a better version of myself.

During this process, you do *not* need to worry about how you might start this business. In fact, this should be a business you specifically do *not* know how to start right now. If you know how to launch it already, it is not a lifting business. It is not even a goal. If you already know how to do it, it's simply an item on your to-do list.

This business needs to be so big that you don't attempt to use your strategies from the past to accomplish it. I want it to be big enough that any old strategies from the past will not work. You must realize that the strategies you used to get you where you are, will be the same strategies that keep you stuck from moving any higher.

Let's compare this to real estate investing. If I set the goal of getting 1000 apartments, it would be illogical for me to try and improve my budget to save up the money to buy them. That strategy would take way too long. I would have to learn new strategies to raise the funds because simply saving money (my old strategy) would limit me from experiencing that type of growth.

Robert Allen famously said, "Everything you want is just outside your comfort zone." I completely agree with this! If you want to experience a big shift in your life, you need a big goal that forces you to step out of your comfort zone and into the unknown.

To help you understand this concept, I want to explain to you what it looks like to "step into the unknown" so that you can see how important this is for your business.

Known Vs Unknown

Most people operate their whole life in the "known." The known is the small section of life that you think you can control. You know what will happen, you know what actions to take, and you know the direction you are headed. If you have been doing the same type of work and living the same type of life for the past ten years, you are living in the known.

If you keep acting out of the known, you will stay stuck in your current reality. It is impossible to accomplish anything new while operating in the known because you are limited to the same inputs you know and have used in the past. If the inputs stay the same, the outputs will stay the same too.

If you want to accomplish something you have never done before, you will need to start looking into the unknown. The unknown is where all the possibilities you do not currently know live. It is where all the knowledge, strategies, people, and ideas that you don't currently know are found.

In order to step into the unknown, you must first reach out to new mentors, listen to new podcasts, read new types of books, go to new networking events, look for new communities to join, visit new places, and take new types of actions. This will help you step beyond your normal "known" reality.

We like to think that we know so much about life, but the reality is, we know only a very small portion of what there is to know. There are experts on topics you aren't even aware of. The unknown has all the strategies, information, opportunities, and connections you need to make your business happen. The unknown is where your great business lives!

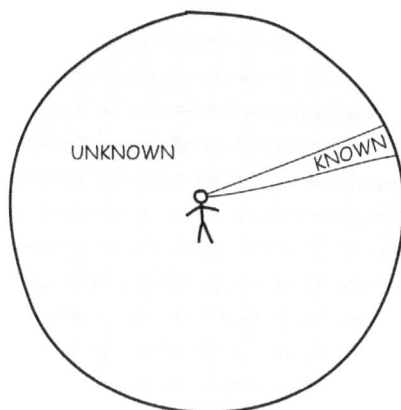

This might be frightening because you cannot control the unknown. You don't know what will happen because you've never done it. However, new inputs will open the doors to getting new results. The unknown is where you meet people that can help you and are introduced to strategies that can change your life.

By aiming for a business that you do *not* know how to accomplish, you are forced to start looking in the unknown. You must take new actions because it is obvious that your old actions will never lead you where you want to go.

Too many people are afraid to do this. They limit themselves to only the business ideas that they currently know how to start. In reality, they are perfectly capable of achieving targets far outside of their current abilities—it will just require them to take new actions.

Don't worry, I will guide you through this process! For now, focus on clarifying a lifting business idea that is desirable enough to motivate you to take new actions, step into the unknown, and become a better version of yourself.

Go through your list and ask yourself if starting this business will hold you back from growing or force you to grow and be lifted. If it will lift you, put an "L" beside it. If you will hold you back, put an "H."

Light

This last step will rely mostly on your gut feeling and intuition. I want you to go through your list of dream businesses and identify which ones feel light or heavy.

Light means it feels exciting and fun. Even if there's going to be a lot of work required for the business idea, there is a natural amount of internal motivation to do it. The idea of pursuing this seems more like play than work and would fill you with energy.

Heavy means the idea of pursuing it seems like a drag. The thought of the business feels tiring, tedious, or demanding. Heavy dreams seem like work and quickly drain you of energy.

For me, the idea of staying at the dealership my whole career felt extremely heavy inside. Even though it was a straightforward path with a very high likelihood of success, it felt heavy! But the idea of starting my planner business, which was much riskier and would require me to work much harder, felt light, filling me with energy and excitement.

Let this be an internal guide to help reveal to you the desires of your heart. Label each business idea with an "L" for light or "H" for heavy.

Don't Worry About Financial Feasibility Yet

You may have noticed that I did not list financial feasibility as one of the criteria. Obviously, generating an income from this business is important, but for now, it is most important to find a passion. I will teach you how to find a profitable business model later.

When I was starting my ecommerce business, I had two friends who each started one that same year. They used the Easy Money approach to find a product to sell online. Neither of them had a product they were interested in, but their financial analysis told them that the products would be profitable. On the other hand their financial analysis showed that my product was likely to fail. I was launching a product in an extremely competitive market with no following of people to sell to.

However, after two years, I was the only business left. All three of us realized it was harder than we expected to start our businesses. This led both of my friends to give up and get jobs again because they didn't have enough passion for the business to figure it out. I put in the work to make mine a success!

I'm not saying you're doomed if you go the Easy Money route. It's just that I truly believe every business can be turned profitable with the right strategies. So, rather than scouring the market for a product that will sell well, scour your heart to find a product or service that will ignite a fire inside you. That is what will increase your chances of success.

You need some level of passion, even if it is for the business process more than for the actual product or service.

For example, I love the process of finding real estate deals and making systems to run them. I view it as a fun puzzle to solve. Although I don't have a passion for apartment style living, I enjoy the process of growing the business. Similarly, you might love the process of finding niche products to sell online. Even if you are not passionate about the products, if you enjoy the process of the business, that will still be enough! The trouble will be if you follow the path my friends did where they didn't have passion for the process or for the products.

Aim to find either a product, service, or business model that sparks a genuine interest of yours.

Choose One

Now that you have gone through your list to add the "L's" and "H's," go through your list again and look for the business ideas that have three L's beside them. If it has three L's, that means "Let's do it!" If it has an "H" beside it, that means "Hold Off."

If you have no business ideas that have three "L's," go back to the prior step and keep listing out business ideas until you find an idea that has all three "L's."

Before we move on, we must narrow this list down to one dream business to pursue this year. Although I would love to see you start many businesses, I do not want you to start more than one business at the same time. I have met way too many people who have tried to start three businesses and fail. The reason they haven't been able to get a single one started is because they created two giant obstacles in the way of getting one done!

Choosing one dream business will narrow your focus and efforts and you will make faster progress. When you narrow your focus to one, you will find that you *can* get your business started this year. Even if it is not a fully formed business idea yet, that is okay.

For example, maybe you want to write a book but you're not sure how to make that a profitable business. That is okay! Choose the dream that has three Ls.

If you have more than one business idea with three "L's" choose the one that seems the most fun. The concept of fun typically encompasses all three "L's." A truly fun activity normally gives us a desire to succeed, challenges us, and feels light. What dream business would be the most fun to start this year?

Your "Why"

Once you choose your business idea, let's start to clarify your "why" behind it. Why do you want this business? Why would it be worth working toward? By taking time to clarify this, you will start to build more internal motivation. I have found that the most successful entrepreneurs have a clear "why" and purpose behind their business. I want you to clarify the same thing.

Here are some questions to help guide you:

- What is your internal motivation for starting this business?
- How will it affect your life?
- What will you have more of?
- What will you have less of?
- How will your business serve others?
- Why would it be worth the time, money, and effort to make this business a reality?
- What new opportunities will be on your horizon after you start this business?

Reflect And Implement

1. Make a list of your dream business ideas. Below are some questions to help:
   - What would be your dream business?
   - What type of business have you always dreamed of having?
   - If you already had tons of money, what business would you start just for fun?
   - What would be a fun way to use your talents?
   - What are the challenges you see others having that you would enjoy helping them overcome?
   - What skills come naturally to you that others struggle with?
   - What have you learned that others can benefit from?
   - What service is lacking in your community that you could provide?
   - What would be a fun way to earn money?
   - What careers have you seen others have that you thought looked enjoyable?

Business Idea	Longing	Lifting	Light
1.	☐	☐	☐
2.	☐	☐	☐
3.	☐	☐	☐
4.	☐	☐	☐
5.	☐	☐	☐
6.	☐	☐	☐
7.	☐	☐	☐
8.	☐	☐	☐
9.	☐	☐	☐
10.	☐	☐	☐
11.	☐	☐	☐
12.	☐	☐	☐
13.	☐	☐	☐
14.	☐	☐	☐
15.	☐	☐	☐
16.	☐	☐	☐
17.	☐	☐	☐
18.	☐	☐	☐
19.	☐	☐	☐
20.	☐	☐	☐

2. Review your list and put a check mark in the "Longing" box by all the ideas that you have a longing for.

3. Put a check mark in the "Lifting" box by all the ideas that are lifting.

4. Add a check mark in the "Light" box by all the ideas that feel light.

5. Identify the business idea that has three check marks beside it. If you have more than one, choose the option that seems the most fun.

6. Now expand on that business idea. Why do you want it?
   - What is your internal motivation for starting this business?
   - How will it affect your life?
   - What will you have more of?
   - What will you have less of?
   - How will your business serve others?
   - Why would it be worth the time, money, and effort to make this business a reality?
   - What new opportunities will be on your horizon after you start this business?

_____

_____

_____

_____

_____

To access a free printout of this exercise, go to **GoalCrazy.com/ freedownloads** or scan the QR code below:

SCAN ME

CHAPTER 5

DAILY DREAMING

While I was in college, I had an extremely unhealthy diet. Lots of pizza, frozen meals, mac and cheese, and Ramen noodles. As you can imagine, I felt terrible basically all the time. I was constantly tired, stomach upset, and felt like I needed tons of caffeine to keep myself awake. After I graduated I started to be more intentional about my diet. I purchased healthier foods like fresh fruit, vegetables, meats, and grains. Almost overnight I felt way better. I felt energized, lighter and happier. Because of this, my wife and I have made it a point to live a healthy lifestyle.

From this experience, I learned a very simple truth. If I eat garbage food, I feel like garbage. If I eat healthy food, I feel healthy. Pretty simple, right?

I bring this up because your mindset works similarly. If you fill your mind with a bunch of negative inputs—worrisome news, insulting self-talk, comparisons to others—you will feel terrible about yourself and have a poor outlook on life. Junk in equals junk out.

Alternatively, if you fill your mind with positive inputs—empowering beliefs, inspiring stories, exciting dreams—you will feel great and have a beautiful outlook on life. Good in equals good out.

Similar to a diet, improving your mindset is not a one-time thing. You don't eat healthy for one day, and then check the "get healthy" box off your to-do list and go back to eating junk. If you want to become healthy, you need to make the commitment to change how you live your life on a daily basis. Your mindset is the same—if you want to improve the way you think, you need to work on it daily! A positive mindset is key for an entrepreneur so they can see opportunities, persevere through difficult times, and confidently take action.

In the previous chapters, you made a dream list and clarified your dream business idea. This is equivalent to going to the store, getting healthy food, and then having your first day of healthy eating. It is a good start, but you need to make dreaming part of your daily life if you want to start thinking like an entrepreneur and experiencing results. Dreaming will not just be a one time thing.

One of my greatest goals with this book is to help you form the habit of dreaming every single day. I have made this part of my life years ago and because of this continued habit I had the clarity, confidence, and energy to start my businesses.

Every morning, I set aside dedicated time just to dream. I go down to our basement, turn on music that inspires me (usually Christian rock), and pace around the room for at least ten minutes, envisioning the life and business I want. I do this every day because it clarifies the life I'm aiming for and fuels the energy to make it happen. That's why I want you to try it too.

Dreaming daily will lead to three things: clarity, an energized mindset, and a stronger dreaming muscle.

1. Clarity

When you start dreaming daily, you get *tons* of clarity. One of the biggest questions I help new entrepreneurs answer is, "What type of business do I want to start?" Whenever I have someone who needs this direction, I always ask them, "What do you dream of doing?"

Some people share with me deep-rooted dreams that fill them with energy that they have never shared with anyone else before. Some people tell me how they have no dreams at all. Most people are somewhere in the middle. Either way, I will tell them the same thing: Start dreaming every day!

If you already have a powerful business dream, thinking about it daily will make it much clearer and stronger. You already have this dream as a flame in your heart and now by dreaming about it daily, you will form it into a raging fire that empowers you to launch it.

If you don't have a powerful business dream yet, daily dreaming will start to show you what ideas are fun to dream about and give you tons of energy. Additionally, you will realize businesses that are *not* fun to dream about and drain you of energy. This will become your guide for what will be rewarding in your actual life.

A few years ago, I coached an entrepreneur who ran two businesses— one was a nonprofit, the other a sprinkler repair company. When he first hired me, he wanted help growing the repair business. But as he began to dream daily, he noticed that all of his dreams revolved around expanding the nonprofit. He found it boring to even think about growing the repair business.

With that insight, we created a plan to sell the sprinkler company and focus entirely on scaling the nonprofit. Once he devoted himself to the mission he was truly passionate about, he grew it faster than expected— and felt far more fulfilled.

You will find similar themes in what you dream about. You will find certain business dreams that come up regularly that you could daydream about all day. You will start to uncover the deeper desires you have in your heart and see how they fit into a bigger purpose for your life.

A dreaming habit will also help you realize when you are off track. If you are currently aiming one direction in life, but dreaming about doing something completely different, you will realize the disconnect sooner. If you don't dream everyday, you won't notice the disconnect and will likely stay on the wrong course longer, leaving you feeling unfulfilled and confused about why you are unhappy.

Because I dream every day, I have a crystal-clear vision of the life I want. That clarity gives me the motivation to push through challenges, because

I know exactly what I'm working toward. That's the kind of clarity I want for you—and the kind you'll gain if you commit to this daily dreaming practice.

2. An Energized Mindset

Dreaming every day is also one of the most powerful methods I have found to improve my mindset. I fill my mind each morning with uplifting thoughts about my life. I dream about what I am capable of, how I can serve others, and how exciting life will be. It gives me a boost of energy as I now see how my actions for the day are moving me in the direction of a life I absolutely love. This opens my mind to find opportunities to make my dreams happen. When I notice these opportunities in my life it makes my dreams even clearer and gives me even more energy to keep dreaming everyday.

Unfortunately, most people do the opposite of this. Rather than dreaming without limits each day, they *worry* without limits. Can you see the trouble with this? If you fill your mind with negative, worrisome inputs, it will drain you of energy and motivation. It will fill your mind with fears which block you from seeing the incredible opportunities in your life.

If you are currently stuck in a funk, need help deciding what to do next, or if you lack motivation, *start dreaming daily*! It will bring you the answers and motivation you need.

3. A Stronger Dreaming Muscle

As you start to dream every single day, it starts to get easier. You will strengthen the creative muscle in your brain to envision a future better than your current reality. You start to see the dreams more clearly and can bring them to the top of your mind at any time.

Just like eating healthier, it may be difficult at first, and it might seem like you have no options of what to eat. But, after committing to it, you will start to find plenty of healthy new choices. You will get better at making healthy meals that taste good, and eventually eating healthier will become easy and natural.

The same is true with your dreams. If you have been struggling to truly clarify your dreams, that doesn't mean you don't have any. It means you need to strengthen your dreaming muscles. Dedicating the time for this daily is the best way to do that. Your mind will naturally start to think bigger and more exciting thoughts habitually.

How To Fit This Into Your Life

I like dreaming first thing in the morning, but pick a time that works well for you. Many people I work with like to dream in the evening to help them wind down, and others in the middle of the day to help keep them focused. All are great options, the key is to have consistency. I want you to look in your calendar over the next 24 hours and find a time you can dedicate ten minutes to dreaming. Then schedule dreaming into your calendar! This is a high-payoff activity.

Don't let the excuse of "not having enough time" stop you. Instead, change that thought to, "How can I create the time for this?" These are your dreams we're talking about—it's worth figuring out. If you can't find just ten minutes to think about your dream business, how do you expect to ever find the time to create it?

During this time, set a timer for ten minutes, turn on music that inspires you, and simply dream. You can sit, stand, lay down, or even walk—whatever feels right for you. Let your body really *feel* what it would be like to live out the dreams. Don't just run through your list of dreams. Find one you like and let it play out in your mind. Experience it! Use some of the questions from the dream list activity if you need a spark of inspiration.

These do not have to be only professional dreams. These can be personal dreams too. Maybe you dream of going to the beach to relax or having a cabin in the woods where you hunt with friends. I will say, if you keep dreaming about having time away from work, that might be a sign you need a break. It might even be an indication that something about your work needs to change. Either way, just let your mind dream without any limits.

This should be time away from distractions when you are completely alone. When do you typically have moments like this during your day? If you don't, how could you adjust your schedule to fit it in? Once you strengthen your dreaming muscle, you can even do this while driving to work, mowing the lawn, or going for a run. Ask yourself, "What activities am I already doing each day that I could pair with dreaming?"

Obviously it is best to have undistracted time to dream so your mind doesn't lose focus, but you can pair dreaming with other activities if that is all the time you have available.

When Distractions Arise

I want to give you a warning for when you first start with this exercise. Distraction will come! Even if you are dreaming completely alone in an undistracted place, your mind will suddenly think of a challenge at work or you will notice a closet in your basement that needs to be organized. It happens. It's okay. You are just getting started with this, and it is normal for your mind to be distracted. When it happens, bring your attention and thoughts back to your dreams. Don't beat yourself up for letting it happen, just start thinking about your dreams again.

If this continues to be an issue, here are a few strategies that can help:

First, get a dream journal. Write in it as if you are a future version of yourself, journaling about a day in your new life. Describe what this future you did that day, the experiences they're having, and the feelings they feel. This exercise helps many people stay focused and gain greater clarity.

Second, use images to support yourself. Print out pictures that represent the life you want to create. We've all heard of a vision board, right? Create one! Get a bulletin board and hang up pictures of things and experiences that inspire you. Use this board as a focal point to keep your thoughts on track.

Reflect And Implement

Schedule your first dreaming session.

When in your day will you fit this in? Where will you go for your dreaming session?(Your room, basement, car, office, etc.)

_____

_____

_____

Commit to doing this every day for at least 30 days. Notice how it shifts your mindset. How does it change how you think of yourself and what is possible in life? View this as an experiment. I am confident if you commit to this for even just one month, you will see shifts in your life and will then want to keep the habit going.

If you need help creating this habit, check out our 30 Days of Dreaming Challenge. You can access the challenge plus download a free guided visualization to help you with this exercise at our site: **GoalCrazy.com/ freedownloads**

Before you move onto the next chapter, set a timer for ten minutes right now and simply dream about the life you want.

CHAPTER 6

CREATE A VISION

There is a scene in the Disney movie *Alice In Wonderland* where Alice is walking through the woods trying to decide which way she wants to go. She sees the cat up in the tree. She asks the Cat, "Can you please tell me which way I should go?"

The Cat replies, "Well that depends on where you want to get to…"

She adds, "Well it really doesn't matter where…"

"Then it really doesn't matter which way you go," finishes the Cat.

Alice says, "So long as I get somewhere!"

"Well you are sure to do that if you only keep walking long enough," responds the Cat.

I bring this up because many entrepreneurs go through life with an attitude similar to Alice's. They tell themselves, "I want my business to go somewhere," but never clarify where. They don't define the type of income they want, the freedoms they expect it to provide, or the time it will require. This lack of clarity causes their business to overwhelm their life.

Recently I worked with an accountant named Tammy who had an accounting firm of her own. She had been working over 80 hours a week for five years, only taking time off in emergencies, and was earning barely enough to cover her bills. She was frustrated because she had successfully accomplished her dream of starting a business, but now felt like a prisoner to it.

For the past five years she had said "yes" to every business opportunity that presented itself, but this led her to being overwhelmed and stuck working all the time. She had customers that paid her to prepare their personal taxes, businesses that relied on her for payroll, high net worth clients that consulted her for financial coaching, and even several other business owners that hired her to set up their accounting software in their office. She was being spread too thin!

David Packard, co-founder of Hewlett-Packard, once said, "More companies die of indigestion than starvation."

I have found this to be so true! I have seen more business owners struggle because they overcommitted themselves than those who struggle because of lack of resources or opportunity. This is exactly the situation that Tammy found herself in, and it almost drove her to quit her dream business out of exhaustion.

The sad thing is, this could have easily been avoided if she had a clearer direction when she started out. Rather than just aiming at "starting a business," a better approach would have been to specify the details of the business.

For example, "I will start an accounting business that will earn me over $250k per year working less than 40 hours per week, with the ability to take six weeks of vacation per year. I will work with small business owners to help them keep their books and run payroll. I will work mostly at the office but have the ability to work remotely two days per week."

If she had this level of clarity it could have guided her to only say "yes" to the business opportunities that aligned with this vision, and the confidence to say "no" to the opportunities that didn't.

It might not seem so now, but if you don't have a clear direction for your new business you can easily fall into a similar situation. When you don't know what you want to do with your life and business, you end up feeling like Alice in a world with lots of different options, only knowing you want to end up "somewhere."

That is why in this next section, we are going to create a clear vision of the lifestyle you want your business to provide.

Your Vision

This vision will be a short description of the type of life you would like to have at a given point of time in the future. Up until now, we have not added a time frame to any of your dreams—they have all been rather vague. Now we will start to clarify a direction for your life so you can use your business to drive it. This will be the first step in turning your dream business into an attainable goal.

You will do this by completing several sentences at the end of the chapter that go something like, "Ten years from now my age will be ___ and my life and business will look like___."

You will create three of these visions.

One for ten years, one for three years, and one for one year.

These visions will be your guide when you are faced with difficult decisions. They will be your "North Star," telling you which way to go. Just like a sailor uses the North Star to guide himself at sea, you will use your vision to guide yourself through life. It will give you a target to aim at and a trajectory to follow.

If you didn't have anything to show you which way was north at sea, it would be very difficult to sail in the right direction. Similarly, if you can't see a clear vision of the life you want in your mind, it will be almost impossible to make it a reality. That's why this is so important!

Each of these are important for different reasons. A ten-year vision is helpful because it allows you to think long-term. Ten years is enough time to radically change your life and yourself.

A three-year vision is also very helpful. It is often said that people overestimate what they can do in one year, but greatly underestimate what they can accomplish in three. Three years gives you a time frame that is close enough to envision clearly, but still enough to make big changes.

A one-year vision is also important because it gives you a short timeframe that drives a sense of urgency. The one year vision for your business will be a powerful driving force to motivate you into action, because the payoff will arrive soon.

I want to remind you again, these visions are not goals. Often when people set long-term goals, they ask themselves, "What is realistic to accomplish over the next ___ years?" However, I want you to focus on, "What would I *love* to accomplish over the next ___ years?"

We will reference these visions in the coming chapters when we set your goals, but you do not need to worry about how you will accomplish them just yet.

My Vision Seems Unrealistic

You might be hesitant to write down anything that seems unrealistic. You probably think, "Why would I write this out if I have no idea how to accomplish it?" Trust me, I thought the same thing. However I want you to realize there is a large factor you haven't considered yet that will make these ambitious visions of yours possible. That is, the power of your skills compounding. Basically, the longer you have a skill, the more powerful it gets.

Let me explain.

Time Value Of Skills

When I was in college, I minored in finance and one of the key concepts we talked about in my classes was the Time Value Of Money. This principle stated that, the longer you have a dollar for, the more valuable it is for you.

Let's say you and your best friend John were walking down the road and a rich man walked up and said he wanted to give you both $100,000. He simply handed John a check for $100,000. But for you, he said he would pay out your $100,000 over the next 20 years. He would pay you $5000 per year so that over the course of the 20 years you would get the full amount.

Who received more value, you or John? John did, of course! But why? You both get $100,000, but John received $100,000 *and* he received the gift of time with it. John can take that money and invest it for 20 years, that way he can have much more than $100,000 in 20 years. If John puts his $100,000 in the bank and earns a five percent interest, he will receive $5000 per year, just like you, *and* have $100,000 in the bank!

You, on the other hand, don't have this same luxury. You have less time with the money to invest and earn from it. The rich man gave you much less.

Actually, the rich man doesn't even have to give you $100,000. If he can get five percent interest on his money, he could leave the $100,000 sitting in his bank account and earn $5000 per year in interest. All he needs to do is give you the interest each year and never actually has to give you the $100,000.

The basic principle is that the longer you have money invested, the more value it gains. Since you'll never be younger than you are right now, it's important to start investing today. It's like that old Chinese proverb: "The best time to plant a tree was 20 years ago. The second best time is now." Investing works the same way—you want to start as soon as possible so your money has more time to grow.

I'm sure you're wondering how this principle applies to your goal of starting a business. It's actually very simple.

Our skills work the same way. The more time you have a skill the more valuable it will be to you. If you learn how to start a business now you will have much more time to use that skill throughout the course of your life. In ten years, you could have used it to start multiple businesses and grow them to a very high level. However, if you wait nine years to get started on your business, you will have the skill for far less time, and therefore not be able to accomplish as much with it. This is the Time Value of Skills, and why *this* year is the best time to start your business and start developing your entrepreneurial skillset.

Let's bring this back to your vision.

Right now, you might write down visions that seem unrealistic, maybe even impossible. But, once you launch your business, learn new skills, and have new resources available to you, the pace at which you can grow will start to increase. It took me almost a year to learn about real estate and buy my first rental property. However, less than five years after that, I grew my portfolio up to over 30 units, simply because my skills started to compound.

Even though my visions seemed crazy when I wrote them down, after I started to accomplish some of my smaller goals, my skills and confidence in myself increased and I started going after larger targets. I gained more resources and connections that made hitting my larger goals easier. Your growth will not be linear—it will be exponential if you follow the processes in this book. When creating visions for yourself, don't worry about making them realistic, focus on creating visions that are motivating.

Reflect And Implement

Complete the three prompts below to create a vision for yourself. For each of these prompts, you can use the questions on the next page to help you think about the different areas of life.

Ten years from now my age will be _____ and my life and business will look like:

_____

_____

_____

_____

_____

Three years from now my age will be _____ and my life and business will look like:

_____

_____

_____

_____

_____

One year from now the date will be _____ and my life and business will look like:

_____

_____

_____

_____

_____

For each area, think about the different areas of life below: (You do *not* need to answer all of these. These are simply to help trigger your imagination.)

Business:

- What will my business look like?
- How much in revenue? Profit? Customer-base size?
- How many hours per week will it require?
- What will my team look like?
- What experiences and opportunities will it be providing to me?
- How much vacation time will it provide?

Health

- What do I want my health to be like?
- What do I want my fitness to be like?
- What will my diet be like?
- How much sleep will I be getting?
- How much stress will I have?

Family and Home

- What will my family life look like?
- How much time will I be spending with my family?
- What activities will we do together?
- What type of home will I have?
- What will my relationship status be?
- What improvement will I have made to the house?
- What new things will I own?

Social

- What type of friends will I have?
- What type of things will I be doing with my friends?
- How often will I see them?

Financial:

- How much will I be earning?
- How much will I have set aside in savings?
- How much passive income will I have?
- How much will I have set aside for retirement?
- How much debt will I have? Will I have any?
- How much will I be giving away?
- What types of things will I now be able to afford?

Personal Development and Education

- What type of person will I become?
- What types of values will I live by?
- What traits will I have?
- What skills will I have learned?
- What will I be doing to improve myself?
- What will I be an expert in?
- How will I feel about myself?

Fun and Travel

- What type of hobbies will I have?
- What will I be doing for fun?
- What type of trips will I be going on?
- How often will I be traveling?

Spiritual

- How will I have grown spiritually?
- How will I be practicing my faith?
- How will I be involved with my church?
- How will I serve God?

To download a free printable PDF of this exercise, go to **GoalCrazy.com/ freedownloads** or scan the QR code below:

PART 2

DESIGN YOUR WINNING PRODUCT OR SERVICE

CHAPTER 7

THE GOAL CRAZY CYCLE™

You are probably wondering, *how*. How will I actually start this business that I have been clarifying? In this next section, I will address exactly that. I will give you the steps you need to get your business kicked off and thriving. I have been able to use these same steps to buy real estate, create my planner business, sell courses, start a coaching company, launch my podcast, and even write this book. This process works!

Not only has it worked for me, it has worked for my clients. It will work for you! Through the years I have had the opportunity to interview over 100 successful entrepreneurs, and they have all used some variation of this process.

I will break down each step so you know how to implement it in your business. Additionally, I will share real world examples of how myself, and clients, have used them so you can have a vision to model.

Let me introduce you to the Goal Crazy Cycle, an easy to use four step process to accomplish any goal.

EXPERT COUNSEL
THE GOAL CRAZY™ CYCLE
REFLECTION
M.I.G.
MESSY ACTION

The first time you go through this cycle, you will use it to design your winning product or service. Then, you will go through the cycle a second time to launch your business.

It might seem like a lot right now, but don't worry—I will lead you through the entire thing.

For this process to work, there's only one thing you must do. You *must* be willing to take action to pursue your business dreams. Up until this point in the book, we have just been clarifying your dreams by performing written activities. In this next part of the book, I will give you action steps to take in the real world, and I need you to make the commitment to yourself to take these actions and pursue your dreams.

Pursue Or Deny

When it comes to the business dreams you clarified, you ultimately have two options. You can pursue your dreams or deny them. There is no middle ground.

If all you do is dream about your dreams but don't pursue them, you are denying them. More importantly, you are denying yourself the opportunity to grow.

Oftentimes, people think that failing is the biggest enemy of their success when the true enemy is being average. There are more people who have given up on their dreams because they settled for average than there are who pursued their dreams and failed. When you deny your dreams, you set yourself on a straight path toward mediocrity. You put yourself on a path of spending your entire life denying your true mission to become great and settle for an average life of comfort.

I don't want that for you! I imagine that if you have made it this far into the book you are not someone whose aspirations are an average, mediocre life. Now that you have taken the actions to clarify your dream business you now know the opportunity that awaits you. You know what is possible, so I want you to pursue your business dreams and nothing less!

Before you continue, ask yourself whether you are going to pursue your dreams or deny them:

- You can pursue your dreams and challenge yourself to grow, or you can deny your dreams and always be stuck in a state of struggle.
- You can pursue your dreams to solve problems for our society or you can deny your dreams and blame others for your problems.
- You can pursue your dreams and take risks to live all out, or you can deny your dreams and avoid risks, which ultimately denies you the freedom to live life at all.
- You can pursue your dreams and have an unstoppable fire of desire and excitement in your heart, or you can deny your dreams and have a heart full of guilt and regret that slows you down.

Which do you want?

I will tell you right now, playing it safe and avoiding action is the riskiest thing you can do. It guarantees you a life of mediocrity that you won't enjoy.

I think we all secretly hope that someone or something is going to come into our life one day and force us to take action, challenge ourselves, push past our fears, and become the best we can be. This business is that opportunity. But you must pursue it!

I want you to realize there will always be excuses to delay taking action. The timing will never seem right, the risks will always seem high, and the challenges will always be there. Deciding to wait is the same as denying your dreams.

There are only two options, deny your dreams and settle for mediocrity, or pursue your dreams, free yourself from your fears, and live all out! The choice is yours. If you are ready to get started, let's dive into the next section of the book so you can learn the proper way to make your dream business happen.

Reflect And Implement

None.

Just get started.

CHAPTER 8

STEP ONE—SEEK EXPERT COUNSEL

When I decided to launch my planner business I had no idea where to start. I didn't know the proper steps to design a winning product or how to get one manufactured. A mentor of mine at the time, Jim Shorkey, reminded me of a very basic math concept that provided me direction. Jim told me, "The shortest distance between two points is a straight line, right? So, the quickest way to launch your business would be to find someone who has already started a similar business, and ask them how they did it. Boom! That will be your straight line!"

It seemed so simple.

I reached out to a friend of mine, named Adam, who had launched multiple online stores to ask for guidance. At the time, I thought my planner design was 100 percent ready to be launched and I just wanted to get advice from him on how to do it. Luckily I showed Adam my design and asked for feedback. He gave me some advice that saved me from having my business totally fail.

Adam recommended I host a focus group to have other people try the planner and give feedback. At the time, I believed it would be a waste of time. Out of respect for him, I hosted one anyway.

To my surprise, the focus group went horribly. Everyone was confused by my design. They kept saying things like, "I'm not sure what I'm supposed to do here," "This feels like too much writing," and "This exercise is repetitive." One piece of negative feedback followed another.

The session was supposed to last 60 minutes but it ended up being over three hours, and we didn't even make it through the entire design. It was painful!

After we were finished, I grabbed my things and went back to my car. I remember sitting there feeling stunned. I thought to myself, "What have I done?" I had left my job and spent months making this planner design that didn't work. I felt embarrassed that I had even shared the design with others. I wanted to give up.

At first, I was angry to have gotten so much negative feedback. I wanted to argue with everyone and convince them their bad opinions of my planner were wrong. After I reflected on the whole thing however, I became grateful for the bad feedback. I also felt relieved I had gotten the feedback now, while I could still easily change the design to fix the issues and avoid terrible reviews from confused customers.

I made adjustments to the planner design based on the feedback and hosted another group. I ended up hosting seven of these groups, making improvements after each one, until eventually I had several groups go through the entire planner and have it work. They would try it out, have wonderful experiences, and more importantly get results!

I can tell you right now, my planner and business would have failed if I hadn't sought advice from an expert like Adam and followed his advice.

This is the power of a good mentor. One piece of advice allowed me to create a successful design and saved me from the humiliation of failure.

I also learned from this experience that most people *want* to help others succeed. Before I met Adam, I was worried he would think less of me because of my lack of knowledge. What I found was that he actually respected me *more* because I admitted my lack of knowledge and sought help.

That is why the first step in this process is to seek expert counsel. I will teach you how to find someone else who has already started a successful business like yours, and ask them how they did it. The goal is to learn from these people how to design a winning product or service with a clear plan to generate profits. They will be able to provide you with the best path toward success and save you years of mistakes. Something that may take you weeks of research they can answer for you in two minutes.

When starting your business, don't ask yourself *how* to start it, rather focus on *who* can help guide you to start it. Everyone gets so fixated on how, how, how, when they should be asking *who*. Who is an expert that you can learn from?

What Is Expert Counsel?

The goal is to find someone you can learn from who has successfully launched a business similar to what you want. I will teach you strategies to find these people, so don't worry right now if you don't know anyone to ask for help. We will refer to these people as "experts."

There are two aspects of good experts:

1. Successfully Similar

Make sure this person is *successfully* doing what you want to do. If you have a cousin who started a business and failed, they will not be the best person to learn from. They will likely give you the wrong advice and possibly even try to talk you out of starting your business to help save you from failure.

The goal is to find successful people to model and learn from. The more similar their business is to yours, the better. If you want to launch an Etsy store selling dog collars, probably finding anyone with a successful Etsy shop will be helpful to learn from, even if they are selling something other than dog collars.

Remember, their advice will lead to a business like their own, so make sure it is one you want to emulate. If they have been in business for five years, work 60+ hours per week, and struggle to pay their bills, their advice and strategies will likely lead to similar results. However, if they have a business that earns consistent profits and requires only 30 hours per week, their advice and strategies will help you do the same.

Look for someone who has a similar business, and has used it to create the lifestyle you want. Those are the best to find!

2. Not Competition

Ideally, you want to find someone you will not be competing with once you start your business. If they view you as a competitor, they will be less likely to share their best strategies. If you want to start a business remodeling kitchens and you have a friend who has the same type of business in your area, you can still ask them for help. But, remember, they will view you as a competitor and will be less likely to openly share. However, if you have a friend who remodels kitchens in another state, or who finishes people's basements, they could be the perfect person to talk to. They can share all the insights they have gained, but will not view you as a competitor.

How To Find Expert Counsel

Now, you might be thinking, "Jason this is great, but I do not know anyone who has started a business like the one I want to start. What do I do then?" I will go over eight different ways to find these people. I will put these in order of the easiest to the most challenging strategies. I highly recommend doing *all* that you can, starting with the easiest, to help build your confidence, then working to the more difficult ones.

When reaching out to these people, you want to find a way to make your meeting mutually beneficial. That way, they *want* to help you. For each strategy, I will share ways to do this and examples of how I have done it within my own businesses.

Approach 1: Friends And Family

The easiest and best place to start is by asking friends and family. If you personally know someone who has started a successful business like the one you want to start, reach out to them, even if you don't have a close personal relationship. One of the first people I reached out to when I wanted to buy rental properties was a past client I had sold a car. I remembered he had rentals, so I reached out to him and asked for advice about real estate investing. I felt nervous calling him because it was outside the scope of our normal car-buying relationship—but I called anyway.

Ask yourself, who do you know who has started a business like the one you want? Make a list and reach out to them. Below is an example of how I would approach the conversation

> *Hey, _____ I hope you are doing well! Right now I am working on getting my first rental property. I remembered you had a number of properties that have done well for you and I wanted to see if I could buy you lunch sometime and consult with you about how you got started? Do you have any availability over the next couple weeks? I would be happy to drive out your way to make things more convenient. I know you are busy, so all good either way, I just figured I would ask, plus it would be great to connect!*

Finding someone you know personally makes things much easier! They are more likely to help you throughout your journey. Them helping you is mutually beneficial because they are given the opportunity to help a friend. I would typically like to at least offer to buy someone lunch or a coffee just to show my appreciation. However, some people are so busy a 15-30 minute phone call might be all they can give you.

If you can't think of anyone you know who is an expert in your desired industry, think about who you know that might know someone who has started a business like the one you want to start. Who do you know that is well connected? Maybe you have a friend who works in marketing and is connected with a bunch of business owners. Maybe you have an uncle who mentioned his friend who has a business. Ask them if they can connect you to the experts you are looking for.

A few years ago, there was a small mobile home park in our area for sale that caught my attention as an investment. The trouble was that I knew absolutely nothing about mobile home parks. Plus, I had never met anyone who owned one. So, I reached out to several of my friends who were well connected in the real estate industry and asked them who they knew who owned mobile home parks. Within a few days I was able to connect with three different mobile home park owners who were extremely helpful. Here is the type of text I sent to find them.

> *Hey _____ hope you are doing well! So, kind of random, but I am looking at buying a mobile home park in our area and I have very little experience in that field. Actually basically none haha! I wanted to see if you knew anyone who had experience owning mobile home parks that you could connect me with? If so, I would love to buy them lunch! However, I imagine they are busy, so even just a 15 minute phone call would be extremely helpful if they would be willing to do it. Do you know anyone that could help?*

The great thing is that even this connection can be mutually beneficial. The expert is ultimately helping the friend that connected the two of you. Similarly, I would at least offer to buy them lunch or a coffee if they are local to your area.

Make a list of who you can reach out to for help. Who do you know that has started a business similar to the one you want to start? Who do you know that is well connected with business owners that they could refer you to?

Approach 2: Networking

The next way to find expert counsel is by finding where these types of experts gather. Look for networking groups, conferences, or trade shows that these people attend. These are goldmines when you can find a gathering of these "experts" together.

I will divide this section into two categories: In person networking and online. Ideally you want to try and meet someone in person if possible. When you meet someone in person the level of connection you have is much higher. If I meet someone, even just on an airplane, I am more willing to give them my contact information than I would if I "met" someone in a Facebook group.

In Person Networking

There are several different tools out there to find communities of experts in your desired industry. A few of my favorites are Meetup, Eventbrite, or Google. Go on these platforms and search keywords related to your industry.

When I wanted to start my ecommerce business, I went to all of these platforms and searched for "ecommerce networking in my area" and found several. At first I was nervous showing up to a random Meetup event where I knew no one. However, once I went there, the people were extremely friendly and helpful. People at these types of events *wanted* to connect with others like myself, that is why they were there. They wanted to learn about my goals and help me.

I also went on Google and searched for ecommerce conferences. Sometimes they are a little harder to find. I like to find books or podcasts for people in my industry and then I will research to see if the author/host puts on events. When I was starting my ecommerce business I researched books on how to start a business online. I then researched the authors and found several who hosted live events and bought a ticket. Not only did I learn a ton at the event, but I met dozens of successful entrepreneurs that I could learn from too.

If you meet experts in person, offer to buy them lunch, coffee, or just have a quick phone call. When I was at these events, I would typically try and find someone to get lunch or dinner with. If they weren't free that day, I would get their contact information to follow up. I would say something like:

> *Hey thank you so much for the advice today, it is extremely helpful. Any chance I could buy you lunch or a coffee sometime this week and chat with you more? I am relatively free Tuesday or Thursday if either of those work for you?*

Or if the person lived out of state:

> *Hey, I would love to connect with you more and see how we can help each other. Would you be free to hop on a quick call later this week?*

People are very quick to hand you their business card. Make sure their cell number is on it. The sooner you follow up with someone the higher the chances are they will take the time to meet with you. Ideally try to schedule a time to talk right when you meet them, but if you can't, I would text them later that same day. If you wait two or three weeks, they will have likely forgotten about you. You need to move as soon as possible.

Spend time researching in-person networking events where your ideal experts go. Register for a few of them and get ready to be social and mingle so you can make the most of your time.

Online Networking

Finding online communities is much easier than finding in-person ones, but it is not always as easy to get the people you meet on the phone with you. However, this is still a very high payoff avenue to pursue. I have become good friends with individuals that I met online and have never actually met in person.

When I was looking at buying the mobile home park, I joined a Facebook group and an online forum for mobile home park owners. Once I was there I posted questions in the groups. In this example the mobile home park I was looking at had a wastewater treatment plant on site, and I was nervous about the expenses of maintaining it. I posted in the online groups,

> *Hello, I am looking at potentially purchasing my first mobile home park in Akron, Ohio. The park I am looking at has a wastewater treatment plant on the premises. Does anyone here have experience with those? Any tips for red flags I should watch for when assessing this deal? They look like they can be pretty expensive to maintain!*

A few people responded to my question. So, for each of the replies I got, I asked the respondent to hop on a call with me. I said something like:

> *Thank you so much! That is really helpful for me. Any chance you would be willing to hop on a quick ten minute phone call to pick your brain on a few things? The whole mobile park world is very new to me.*

I have found this approach works well. First, post a question that is easy for people to reply to, then follow up with the respondents to see if they will hop on a call with you. If they live in the area, I offer to buy them lunch.

To find these groups, research "communities for _____" and list the type of expert you are trying to find. For example, I searched, "communities for mobile home park owners." Maybe you are searching for roofers, ecommerce store owners, or authors.

Next, look for Facebook Groups, blogs, forums, Reddit threads, or associations. Find a few to join and start making posts. Some communities are very active with great participation, and others are not. So, post in a few until you get replies, then ask the people who reply to hop on a quick call with you.

Approach 3: Cold Call

The third option is simply cold calling the experts you want to talk with. Now, I know cold calling gets a bad rap, but this method *does* work! When I wanted to buy a mobile home park I cold called the other mobile home parks in the area and asked to speak with the owner. Most of the places I called didn't answer or told me they weren't available to talk. Several of the others were extremely helpful. They shared key points to research, contacts in the industry, and information about vendors they use. It was amazing!

This strategy works best when you connect with business experts in your industry who aren't direct competitors and when you have specific, quick questions to ask. A question that might take you weeks to research could take them just a couple of minutes to answer. For example, when I called other property owners, they quickly provided information that would have been difficult for me to find on my own, such as:

> *Hey, I saw you have a wastewater treatment plant at your park. I wanted to see which company you use to service it? I am looking at buying a mobile home park in the area and need help finding good options to use for the maintenance.*

If the person seems helpful and we easily connect on the phone, I will offer to buy them lunch or schedule a meeting together. However, often a free lunch is not enticing enough for someone to give time away to a stranger who cold called them.

Another trick to get these people to help is finding a way to make it mutually beneficial. If you are asking for more than just two minutes of their time, they will start to think, "What's in this for me?" You can offer a way to collaborate with them. This will probably be easier once you get your business started but can still be a viable option before.

For example, if you are starting a plumbing business, you could cold call an HVAC company and offer to collaborate. That way it becomes a win-win for you both.

> *Hey my name is _____, I am starting a plumbing business in the area and I figured we might be able to help each other out since our customers can likely benefit from each other's services. I wanted to see if I could buy you lunch sometime and learn about your business.*

When I was starting my planner business, I emailed a few other online stores that sold products for business owners and offered them a free planner in exchange for feedback.

> *Hey, my name is Jason, I am launching a planner that helps entrepreneurs set goals. I thought it would be a helpful tool for you since it aligns with your business mission. I wanted to see if I could send you a free copy and get your feedback on it. I am trying to make it the best it can be, and insights from an expert like yourself would be extremely helpful.*

Now that I have a podcast, I do this literally all the time! I can reach out to authors, speakers, and business owners I want to connect with and invite them to be guests on my show. It's helpful for me because I get to pick their brain for an hour, and it's helpful for them because they get to market their expertise to my audience.

The more you can make the interaction a win for them, the more likely they will be willing to do it.

If the thought of cold calling makes you nervous, remember that the worst-case scenario is simply a "no." Consider starting with a low-stakes business to practice calling and then work your way up to the higher-stakes opportunities. For example, you could reach out to the YouTuber that has 200 followers first and then work your way up to reaching out to the ones with 100,000.

Now let's implement this. What are some businesses that can help you? What are some businesses that are in a similar space, but will not be your competitors? Brainstorm how you can make their collaboration a win-win for both of you. Find their contact information and call them. If you can't find a phone number, send them an email.

Approach 4: Connect With Target Customer

Another method to find experts is to connect with your ideal customers. Meet with your target customers to explain or show the product or service you are wanting to bring to market and ask for feedback. When I was launching my planner business, I met with a few people I knew who were "planner addicts" that had tried dozens of different planners. I was able to ask them about their experiences, what they liked and didn't like, and learn valuable insights. I was also able to show them my planner design and have them give me beneficial feedback on it.

Here is a sample text I used to connect with planner lovers:

> *Hey I hope you are doing well! So, I remembered that you are someone who loves planners and have tried a whole bunch of them. I am currently designing my own! I wanted to see if you would be willing to let me buy you coffee or a lunch and ask you about what you look for in a planner? Any feedback you have will be extremely helpful for me as I put my design together.*

If you were starting a bed and breakfast, it would probably be helpful to talk with people who stay in B&Bs regularly, so you can learn from them what they look for when choosing a place. If you are launching a board game, it would be extremely helpful to talk with someone who plays a lot of board games and get their advice.

Think about who you know that regularly uses products or services like the one you're creating. Where do these types of customers gather? Where can you find them? If you don't know any, use the networking strategies mentioned in Approach Two to locate them. Just as there are communities of business owners, there are communities of similar customers both online and in person. Find where they gather, and go there to meet them.

Multiply Your Experts

With each strategy I have listed, whenever you find someone that is helpful, ask them for referrals. Ask them who they know that would also be helpful for you to connect with. Remember, typically business owners are friends with each other. Now that I am a full time entrepreneur, most of my closest friends are also business owners too. It's just part of human nature, we tend to surround ourselves with people similar to us. Often when I met one "planner lover," they would know a bunch of friends who also had a planner obsession too.

Once you find a helpful expert in your industry, simply ask:

> *Who else do you know that you think could be helpful for me to meet with?*

Then be sure to follow up with the leads they give you!

Approach 5: Vendors

This fifth approach, I have put further down the list because, although it is one of the easiest, it will not always be the most effective.

Think of the vendors that business owners in your industry use and call them. For example, if you want to buy rental properties, you could call real estate agents. The real estate agents are very likely to answer the phone since they are in sales and they know a lot about the industry. They have lots of connections in the space and know common practices.

When I was interested in buying the mobile home park, I called the mobile home dealers in the area and asked for advice. They weren't actually mobile home park owners, but they still provided a lot of information. When I was curious about ecommerce, I called several of the software companies that ecommerce store owners would use. The salesman I spoke with did not own a company himself, but he was able to tell me many common practices in the industry.

Remember though, these people you talk to are salesmen. It's not that they are dishonest, but they will only be talking to you about the easy, quick, fun parts of the business. They will make it seem like running a business is a breeze (as long as you use their product or service). However, they can still teach you a ton of great insights.

Ask yourself what software, vendors, contractors, or companies your ideal expert would be working with. Make a list and call them. This strategy works best when you are seeking answers to specific questions and are truly in the market for what they sell. This makes the relationship a win-win. They will help you in exchange for you giving them a shot at selling you.

When I hired my first employee, I wasn't sure where to start. There are a lot of legal and tax procedures to go through and I wasn't sure what to do first. I knew I would need some sort of payroll software, so I called half a dozen of them and asked for help. This is what I said:

> *Hey, I am looking to hire my first employee and I need help learning where to start. It looks like there are a lot of forms I need to fill out and file with the government. I wanted to see what the steps are to get set up as an employer, and which of these steps your software will help me with compared to which I will need to do on my own? Can you give me some guidance?*

After a handful of these conversations, the steps became very clear for what all I needed to do for my business. Obviously, do not substitute calling vendors for proper legal advice when setting something like this up. I used this just to gather basic guidance and to help decide which software to buy.

Depending on the situation, you can even ask for references of customers to speak to. For example, when I was looking for a digital marketing agency for my online business, I asked the salesperson if they had any past clients I could speak with about their experience working with their marketing agency. They connected me with several, all of which were some of their most successful clients. If they connect you with a client, it will likely be one of their high performers to help make them look good. This was great for me! I was able to ask the client about their experience with the marketing agency *and* learn about how they ran their business.

Now, I don't want you to do anything unethical here, like calling companies that you never intend to use or manipulating others to provide you with contacts. However, if you are genuinely interested in what they provide, it is a great bonus.

So, start thinking, what are some of the vendors, software, or providers business owners in your industry work with? Which of them might be able to help give you helpful insights into how to start your business? Give them a call. If they seem helpful, ask for references for some of their clients!

Approach 6: Find Businesses For Sale

Wouldn't it be convenient if a successful business owner opened up their books and explained exactly how their whole business worked? Well, you can often experience this if you find a business listed for sale. You can find businesses similar to yours for sale on websites like BizBuySell, BizQuest, or Flippa. You can then have access to speak with the owner or broker about how the business operates. You can even learn helpful information about the business just from the business listing. You might even find the perfect business opportunity to buy rather than starting your own from scratch!

You can additionally research franchise opportunities in your industry using the same websites listed above, or Google. Find franchises for sale in your niche, and schedule a call to learn from them about their business model.

I don't want you to completely waste these people's time, so I recommend this approach mainly to someone who is debating whether to buy an existing business or start their own. I also recommend you be upfront about your intentions if you use this approach. For example, you could tell the seller:

> *Hey _____, I saw your business for sale and am very interested to learn more about it. I would love to own a business like this and am trying to decide between buying an existing one or starting my own from scratch. It seems like buying yours could save me years of work, so I would love to ask you a few questions so I could understand how your business operates and see if it fits what I am looking for.*

Depending on the business opportunity for sale, you will likely need to sign a Non-Disclosure Agreement before accessing any of the detailed information to make sure you will not share any of their details or trade secrets. I am not advising you to steal someone else's trade secrets and then use them to launch a competing brand. That would be unethical and likely illegal. I am presenting it as an opportunity to learn basic processes in the industry while comparing the opportunity of buying an existing business to starting one from scratch.

When I was wanting to grow an email list for my online business, I researched several brands for sale in my niche that had a large email list. I wanted to compare the process of building my own email list to buying another brand that had one in place. I ultimately decided to build my own, but I was able to learn several successful strategies of how to do it from researching the brands for sale.

Approach 7: Learn Without Meeting

This approach allows you to learn from experts without actually speaking with them. There are incredibly smart, successful people out there, and fortunately, many have written books! For only $15 (give or take), you can buy a book and learn their philosophies for business and life.

When getting started in a new business, or working to grow your own, you should find books, podcasts, courses, YouTube channels, social media profiles, or any source to learn from these experts. Obviously you are already reading a book about how to start a business, but this should not be the only book you read. Make a commitment to learn every day. The more you surround yourself with strategies and stories of people becoming successful in your industry, the more confidence you will have to become successful too.

I personally believe books are one of the best ways to learn. Podcasts, Youtube channels, and TikTok are really great, but to get the full picture, books are the place to go. Research books in your industry, and make the commitment to read regularly.

Approach 8: Hire A Coach

This approach should be the most helpful, the fastest, and possibly even the easiest to find. However, it will cost you money! Rather than trying to meet experts who will help you for free, you can find coaches within your industry. My favorite way to do this is find books very targeted toward the business you are trying to start. If you are trying to start a podcast, you can research books specifically for starting a podcast. Then, research the author and see if they have any coaching programs.

Additionally, you can simply search on google for coaches in your industry. However, the benefit of finding their book first, is that you can read their book and see if you like their strategy before actually getting started with them.

A good coach should tell you the exact steps you need to take and help hold you accountable to make it happen. Additionally, a coaching program can likely connect you with other similar entrepreneurs. You can meet other people who are on the same journey at different levels. I have hired many coaches to help me with my businesses, and although I learn a lot from the coaches themselves, I often learn just as much from the other clients in the program that I connect with.

If you have a tight budget, try and use all the free approaches first and turn only to paid options if you still need help. But if you are in a hurry to get your business started and/or have a flexible budget, this is the fastest option, as long as you hire a good coach.

For example, as I am writing this book, I hired a coach to help. Having a coach has been able to shortcut my progress. They can give me personal feedback for my situation and hold me accountable to take the actions I need to. I knew that once I cut the check to pay the coach, I had full confidence my book would happen because they would make sure of it.

Connect With Several Experts

Use these strategies to connect with several experts in your business niche. Each person will have different approaches and will have new tips to share. I would aim to meet with at least three. If it is a complex business you want to start, you may want to meet with many more until you have a decent understanding for how to start the business.

Meeting with several entrepreneurs will also help you see through the "fluff." The reality is, most people only want to share the best aspects of their business. Even if their business is barely getting by, they will likely tell you it is great. By meeting with several people, you will start to be able to get a better sense of who is running a business effectively and who is not. This will help you better decide which of the advice to follow.

When I started buying rental properties, I met with several different landlords. A few of them I could quickly tell were extremely organized with their business. They had written processes to handle the demands of the business which made it much smoother to run and scale. However, several others, I could tell, were very unorganized. Although they had a cash flowing portfolio of rentals, they had much more of a "let's see what happens" approach. I could tell their business required much more work from them because they didn't have processes to handle problems as they arise.

The reality is, both approaches were helpful to learn from. I could immediately see the value of streamlining processes right at the start of my business. However, seeing the entrepreneurs with a much more relaxed approach also helped give me confidence to start. I learned it was okay if my processes weren't perfect, because they were succeeding and appeared to have no processes at all!

What If I Have No Clue What To Do?

Maybe you are still unsure of the exact business you want to start. In that case, this step is still helpful to gain more clarity.

Ask yourself, who do you admire? Who has a business and life that you would love to emulate? Offer to buy that person a lunch. Be upfront about the position you are in, and seek their guidance. Don't expect them to solve your life for you, or to tell you exactly what to do, but ask for guidance. Try this phrasing:

> "Hey _____, I want to start a business this year and need some guidance. I have a few business ideas in my head, but basically I have no clue where to start haha. I know you have started a successful company, and I wanted to see if I could chat with you for advice? Would you be willing to let me buy you lunch or a coffee sometime and ask you a few questions? Any advice you have would be really helpful!"

Ask others for help and let them help you. You will be surprised by the opportunities that arise. Often people have too much pride to admit they need help to others. If this is you, don't let your pride get in the way of the incredible business you can have!

Reflect And Implement

Let's implement this so you can connect with helpful experts in your industry. Start by making a list of the potential experts that you can reach out to:

- Which friends and family members have started a business similar to the one you want to start?
- Who do you know that is connected to owners of businesses like the one you want to start?
- What are some in-person and online communities that you can join where you can connect with entrepreneurs in your industry?
- What are some businesses similar to the one you want to start that you can cold call? What are some ways you can make this conversation mutually beneficial?
- Who do you know that is a customer to businesses like the one you want to start? Who uses services and products like the one you are developing?
- What software, vendors, and third party companies would businesses in your industry likely use that you can reach out to?
- What businesses are for sale in your space that you could learn from?
- What are the books, podcasts, and YouTube channels that teach how to start a business like the one you want?
- Who are some coaches that work with entrepreneurs in your specific industry that can help you launch your business?

_____

_____

_____

_____

_____

_____

After you create your list, reach out to them! These people will provide you with the quickest way toward your dream business. Decide how many you can reach out to this week. Use the templates messages I provided to text, call, or email these people to schedule a time to talk.

If you need help creating your list of experts, download our Expert Council Compilation PDF to guide you. You can access it for free at **GoalCrazy.com/freedownloads** or by scanning the QR code below:

CHAPTER 9

THE WINNING PRODUCT OR SERVICE BLUEPRINT

Now that you have a list of experts to connect with, and hopefully some meetings scheduled, it is time to start to plan how that conversation will flow. These experts have the answers you are looking for, and with the right questions you can gather them.

To help you prepare for this conversation with them, I want to break down the process of designing a winning product or service. That way, you will be able to ask educated questions to your experts. I will explain each of the steps required to design a winning product or service, then for each section I will provide a list of questions to guide you on what to ask your expert counsel.

You do *not* need to ask all the questions I provide in this section. These are just examples to help you clarify the most important questions to ask. I want you to think of your time with your experts similarly to time spent with a lawyer. Lawyers charge anywhere from $100-$500 per hour. In some cases more! Just think, if someone was going to charge you $500 per hour, you would likely narrow your questions to the most important ones to ask them before meeting, right? That is what I want you to do before you meet with your experts.

To help you identify the high impact questions most relevant for you, I have included our Winning Product or Service Blueprint at the end of the chapter (you can also download a PDF version of this at **GoalCrazy.**

com/freedownloads). Use the strategies from this chapter to fill out the blueprint. Then identify the areas of the blueprint you are unsure of to discuss with experts for advice.

Let's start by defining what a winning product or service is. A "winning" product or service has two primary components:

1. It solves a genuine problem the customer has.
2. You can earn a profit selling it.

You need both! A perfect product will fail if people aren't willing to pay profitable prices for it. A highly profitable product will fail if no one wants it. You need a product people desire *and* that they are willing to pay profitable prices for.

To design this winning product/service for yourself, you will take the business idea you generated in Chapter Four and clarify three additional pieces of information from it. The Who, What, and How. That is, *Who* is your customer, *What* problem do they have, *How* much are they willing to pay to fix it?

Who Is Your Customer

The first thing we need to clarify is your customer. What type of people would you like to serve with your business idea from Chapter 5? Think about the age, gender, location, income level, occupation, marital status, interests, etc.

This might sound crazy, but the more niche your target customer is, the better. If you believe your target customer is "everyone," niche down further. It will be way too hard to market to everyone. Imagine if you were trying to launch a podcast and you were going to make helpful content for everyone. It would be extremely difficult to separate yourself from the competition. People have almost unlimited podcasts to choose from. It would be hard to write attention catching headlines that attract listeners.

However, if you niched your content down—for example, to men over the age of 50 who play pickleball, then it would be much easier. There is much less competition in a small niche like that. You could write headlines, discuss challenges, and share strategies that speak directly to that person. You will get listeners saying things like, "I feel like this show was made for me!"

Obviously women or younger people could listen to the show too, but the tight focus on a niche allows you to become an expert on a specific topic and to build a passionate following. That is the type of target customer you want.

Think for yourself:

- Who is my ideal customer?
- Who do I want to help with this business?
- What is the age, gender, location, interests, income level, occupation, hobbies, marital status of my ideal customer?

What Problem Of Theirs Will You Solve

Next, we need to understand the problem your customer has. Customers ultimately buy things to solve problems. Yes, they do buy things that they want, but the underlying desire comes from a problem that needs solving. If someone does not perceive they have a problem, they will not be willing to pay for a solution.

One common expression in marketing is to "sell pain pills not vitamins." They say this to communicate the importance of solving a painful problem for the customer. Most people know that vitamins are healthy, but people regularly forget to take them because they don't solve an immediate problem. It might take years of taking vitamins consistently to see results in your health. However, if you are experiencing pain and take a pain pill, your pain is relieved almost immediately. If you have intense pain, you will buy expensive pain pills and set alarms so you remember to take them. That is the type of dedication you want your customers to have to your product or service.

Even people who buy expensive cars, high-end watches, or luxury items are solving problems. They might have the problem of feeling inadequate so they buy fancy items to prove their worth. They might have the problem that their neighbors have nicer things than them, so they want to fix this "problem" by purchasing new items. These are just some examples—obviously there are various reasons, but the point is that customers pay to have problems solved.

The bigger the problem your product will solve, the higher the demand will be for your service. Once you clarify what the customer's problem is, you will be able to position your business as the solution to their problem.

Reflect and use the questions below to identify the pain points your customer has:

- What problem is your customer currently facing that your business will help them solve?
- What pain point do they have?
- What is the end outcome your target customer desires that you can help them achieve?

It is helpful to meet with your target customers and ask them for guidance. They will be experts on the problems customers regularly face with the current solutions. Plus, they can provide valuable feedback on your own product/service. If you are unable to find customers to meet with, you can often find their feedback online.

Look up competitors who have a similar product or service to the one you are creating. Look at their customer reviews. Look at the five star reviews to learn what is important to the customer, then also look at the one star reviews to find problems customers are having with the current solutions.

Questions to ask target customers:

- What problems are you currently facing with the available solutions?
- What do you look for when shopping for a product or service like this?

- What do you think of the current design I have? How do you think I could make it better?
- What do you like best about your current solution?
- How much are you currently paying for the solutions you have?
- How much more would you be willing to pay to have my unique benefits?

How Much Are They Willing To Pay To Solve The Problem

When designing your product or service it is important to know roughly what you can charge for it. You obviously want to make sure you can sell it for more than the costs. There are four easy steps to do this:

1. Research your price points.
2. Find backend upselling opportunities.
3. Total your costs.
4. Calculate your profitability.

Research Your Price Point

When trying to determine the price point of your product or service, think about the benefits your product or service provides. What is it worth to the customer to fix the problem that they have? Obviously you can change your prices and experiment with them to find the sweet spot once you launch your business. At this point, we just want to get a rough idea of the price points to make sure you can earn a profit.

An easy way to do this is to look at what your competitors are charging for similar products or services. Go to Google and look online at your competitors' websites. If needed, call their company and ask questions. You can also get a relatively fair idea by asking AI tools like ChatGPT for average price points in your industry or location. Obviously not everything AI says is 100 percent accurate, but it can give you a baseline idea to start with. The best strategies however, will come from talking with your experts, so I will provide a list of questions to help at the end of this section.

Find Backend Upselling Opportunities

Not only do you need to understand the pricing for your business, you must know how you will be able to earn a profit. You need to understand the business model behind the product or service. For many businesses, the model may be pretty obvious and straightforward. For example, with my planner business, I have suppliers manufacture the planners and then I sell them at a profit. However, other businesses might be a little less obvious, such as if you want to start a blog or podcast.

You might not realize right away how those generate revenue. Either way, you need to learn the model of how your business will earn you money. Not that I want this business to be solely about the money, but revenue is the lifeblood of your business. Without revenue, and more importantly profit, your business will die.

A big part of many business models are backend products. Many businesses have products they sell upfront that generate revenue, but earn most of their profits on the upsells. For example movie theaters sell tickets, but earn most of their profits by upselling food and drinks at their concession stand. I recently learned after speaking with many authors that most of their income does not come from their books, but rather the speaking gigs, conferences, consulting, and courses they sell on the backend of the book.

If there are backend opportunities for you to earn money in your business, you will want to learn these upfront so you can build them into your business model. The best place you can learn these is your experts or target customers. Additionally, you can shop your competitors to see what they are doing. Or a less accurate, but quick option is to ask an AI platform, "What are potential upsells I could sell my customers who purchase _____ from me?"

Calculate Your Costs

After you determine the price, you also want to learn the costs. If it is a product, you need to learn what your cost of inventory will be, and if it is a service based business you need to calculate the cost of supplies and labor. This is another key area for expert counsel because there might be costs you are unaware of that they can bring to light, or teach you strategies to greatly reduce.

You can also start doing research on your own by contacting suppliers. Often, suppliers are experts in your industry too, who you can ask for recommendations or advice.

Determine Your Profitability

Once you have the price point and upselling opportunities, you can calculate your gross profit by subtracting your costs from the sale amount. Make sure the amount of profit is worth your while, and don't just look at the profit margin (profit per sale divided by selling price). Look at what the dollar figure is for each sale. For example, if you are selling a one dollar product that only costs you one cent to make and sell, you will have a 99 percent profit margin. However, you are still only making $0.99 per sale. You would have to sell thousands per month to make it worth your while. Compare that to selling a $1000 product that costs you $500—now you have a 50 percent profit margin, but you profit $500 per sale. Even if you only sell twenty per month, you still earn $10,000!

If you find you aren't able to turn a profit, you will need to either research ways to increase the revenue (ex: charge higher prices, offer more upsells, etc.) or reduce expenses. This is where an expert can be an extremely helpful guide.

If the experts and data all tell you profit is not possible, you may need to go back to Chapter Four and pick a new business idea.

Questions To Ask Your Experts

Now that you have a rough idea how to research the pricing and costs for your product, here are some example questions you can ask your experts to best do this for your business:

- How niche should my target customer be? How can I find them?

- How can I find the problems they have that my business will solve?
- How should I price my products?
- How did you price your products?
- What softwares, tools, or strategies have you used to determine the optimal price to charge?
- Are there backend products or upsells that you offer after your initial sale?
- What percentage of customers buy the upsell?
- How do you determine the best price points for your backend products?
- What are your costs associated with each sale? How much are they?
- How am I able to learn what my costs would be? Are there tools or contacts you would recommend?
- Are there suppliers you recommend to get your supplies or inventory?
- How will I generate profit from this business?

Design Your MVP

After you define your target customer, you need to design the product or service that will solve their problem. You will need to design your Minimum Viable Product (MVP) – that is the basic version of your product or service that you can sell and start testing the market with. This does not need to be the finalized product or service. It can be a prototype, mockup, or draft version. We simply need a basic version of your product that you can use to test the market with and validate your business idea is a winner before you spend time and money launching it. Creating this MVP needs to be the primary focus for your business right now, because unless you have a product or service to sell, nothing else for your business will be relevant.

A few years ago, I was working with a friend who designed a protein bar to sell for people with specific food allergies. She was working on the packaging for the bars, a website, logo, and Facebook ads for her business. I reminded her that she hadn't even made the bars yet! Plus, she wasn't sure if the market wanted them. I reminded her to narrow her focus to making her first batch of these bars to test the market with. Until she had them, nothing else for her business would be relevant.

I will warn you, it's easy to fall into a similar trap. When starting your business it is easy to get distracted with many of the other activities involved and lose focus of your MVP. I meet people all the time who have an idea for a business, but rather than finishing their product design, they start making a website, logo, LLC, business cards, social media page, etc. Look, those things are helpful, but they will be useless if you never have a product to sell! You *must* have a basic version of your product or service established for any of those other things to even be relevant. The most beautifully designed website will be meaningless if you have nothing to sell on it.

This is important for service based businesses too. For the service you could at least create a proposal, flyer or sales pitch that clearly outlines what service you are providing to test the market with. For example, if you wanted to start a business cleaning windows, all you need is a sales pitch and you could start testing the market to see if people are even interested in your service.

Ask yourself now, what is your Minimum Viable Product? What is a simple version of your product or service that you can create to test the market with? It could be a sample, mockup, proposal, prototype, or simply a sales pitch.

Your experts will be able to provide the best advice for how to design your unique product or service for your market. They will know the processes, suppliers, and contacts that will make it easy. Below are a list of questions to ask these experts to help give you guidance.

Questions to ask experts in your industry:

- How did you design the first version of your product/service?
- How did you incorporate the needs of your customers into the design?

- How did you make your product/service unique?
- What has made your product/service to be a success?
- What do you think of my current product/service design?
- How do you think I could make my idea even better?
- Is there anything you would do differently?

Use these as a reference to create a list of questions you can ask your experts to learn the best strategies for creating a profitable, winning product or service.

As you ask these questions, be open to receiving negative feedback. You may disagree with the feedback your experts give you. I cannot guarantee that it is 100 percent correct, but if you have several people telling you the same thing, I would listen. There have been many times I was super excited about a business idea that I thought was great, but then several mentors of mine told me it was terrible. At first I was angry and my pride wanted to disagree with them. But looking back, following their guidance has led me to much better opportunities.

Reflect And Implement

Below is our Winning Product/Service Blueprint. Fill out as much as you can then make a list of questions to ask your experts to learn the best strategies for the areas you are unsure about.

Winning Product or Service Blueprint

Who

Who is your target customer? What is their age, gender, income level, location, age, interests, etc.?

_____

_____

_____

_____

What

What is your customer's problem that your business will solve?

_____

_____

_____

_____

How

How much will you charge for your product or service?

_____

_____

_____

_____

What are the backend products you can sell? How much can you charge for them? How often do you expect customers to buy them?

_____

_____

_____

_____

What are your costs associated with your product or service? How much are they?

_____

_____

_____

_____

How much profit will you generate from a sale? Is it enough to justify your efforts?

_____

_____

_____

_____

What is your Minimum Viable Product (MVP)? (examples: a sample, prototype, mockup, or even a sales pitch to test the market with for your product or service) How will you make it?

_____

_____

_____

_____

You can download a PDF version of this, plus a compiled sample list of questions to ask your experts, at **GoalCrazy.com/freedownloads** or by scanning the QR code below:

CHAPTER 10

VALIDATE YOUR BUSINESS IDEA

With your MVP designed, and a basic idea of how this business can earn money, it's now time to test the idea out in the marketplace to validate it. This step is *key*! Before you spend time and money building out the rest of your business to launch, make sure your product is ready and desirable from your target market. Simply having people tell you it is a good business idea is not enough. You want to test the product or service in the marketplace to make sure it is a winner.

To do this, we need to make sure it completes our "winning product" criteria listed earlier:

1. It solves a genuine problem the customer has.
2. You can earn a profit selling it.

We will call this process validation. There are many different ways to do this, but I will show you four basic strategies to implement this. The best strategies however, will come from your expert council, so use this as a basic framework to ask quality questions to learn from them. The four validation strategies are: Beta Testers, Focus Groups, Surveys, and Pre-sales.

Beta Testers

One of the first methods you can use is offering your product or service for free—or at a significantly reduced price—in exchange for feedback. You might ask experts in your field to try it, or you could reach out directly to your target customers. Both groups can offer valuable insights.

If you receive negative feedback, you'll gain a clear list of improvements to make before your official launch. If the feedback is positive, you can use those responses as testimonials to help drive sales.

For example, when I was preparing to launch a course, I offered a select group of people free access in exchange for their feedback. Their input helped me clarify confusing sections and remove parts that felt repetitive. It was incredibly helpful!

If you want to launch a business of your own, think of ways you can have people try your product or service before selling it. For example, my friend who was designing the organic protein bar could give samples out to her target market for free in exchange for their feedback. If you wanted to start a business designing websites, you could offer to design a friend's website for free (or at a reduced price), to test out the quality of your work, and get a customer review.

After they try your product or service, survey them for what they would be willing to pay for it. Ask them for a suggested price point they think it is worth.

Focus Groups

Another easy way to validate a product or service is to host a "focus group." Gather a group of your target customers together to try your product or service and provide feedback. This is the method I used to gain valuable insights on my planner design. I have found that when you meet with people one-on-one and ask for feedback, they are often afraid to share anything negative. Although, when you put people in a group, they are much more likely to share what they honestly think. Positive feedback and negative feedback. You would much rather know any problems with your design before you launch when it is easy to fix rather than waiting until after you launch and get negative feedback in the form of poor customer reviews.

The easiest way to host a focus group is to invite a small group of friends and family who fit your target market together. Show them your product or service and ask for feedback about each aspect of your design, both good and bad. What do they like? What is confusing?

If you get negative feedback, address the concerns and host another focus group to test the improved design. Keep doing this until you have positive experiences. This will give you confidence to know you have a winning business idea before you launch.

Hosting this group in person is ideal, but if that is not possible, this can be done online too. Over the years I have mailed out samples of new planner variations to customers and then had them participate in a virtual focus group to learn their feedback.

Lastly, you can ask your participants about the pricing. You can ask what they believe a fair price would be for your product or service.

Surveys

Another way to gain feedback from your target market is through market research surveys. I've met entrepreneurs who sent out surveys to a large group of their target market to get feedback and test the demand. This can give you quantitative data to help inform your decisions.

It's very easy to do this if you already have an email list or social media following. You can create a survey that will test the demand of your product or service. You can use a tool like Google Forms to create the survey for free!

Even if you don't have a large following, you can tap into your personal network. Pull out your phone and look how many contacts you have saved in there–probably hundreds! Look how many followers do you have on social media—likely hundreds more. Reach out to them and ask for their input on your survey.

Additionally, there are many websites where you can pay to survey targeted groups of people too. Some of my favorites are Pickfu.com or Pollfish.com. Both of these are relatively inexpensive and make it easy to create a survey.

For only a few hundred dollars I was able to survey a targeted group of people to find the most appealing subtitle for this book.

Just like the other approaches, you can survey the market for price points with these surveys too.

Pre-Sale

A mentor of mine, Chandler Bolt, has said repeatedly that "people vote with their wallet." This means you don't just need people to tell you they like your idea, you need them to actually take money out of their pocket and buy it. That is the true proof of whether they think it is a good idea. If people aren't willing to do that, it means there is still something wrong with the design. This is the idea behind the pre-sell strategy.

Find a way to presell your product or services to people to see if they are truly interested. When I was launching my planner business, I sent out an email similar to this:

> *Hey Sam,*
>
> *The past few months I have been designing a planner to help high achievers like yourself accomplish their goals. I have spent over six months interviewing successful entrepreneurs and hosting focus groups to nail down a design, and I finally made one that is getting incredible results!*
>
> *I am having a small batch of these planners printed and I thought you might enjoy one. If you would like one, go ahead and Venmo me $20 this week so I can make sure you get a copy. I plan to sell them for $35, but for this first order they will be discounted.*
>
> *Thanks,*
>
> *Jason V.*

This helped me validate that people truly were willing to pay for my planner before spending thousands of dollars having them manufactured.

You can do this for service based businesses too! I worked with an entrepreneur who wanted to start a business power washing houses. He saw several people on TikTok doing it and thought it seemed like a fun business. He told me how he was going to buy a power washer, cleaning supplies, and hoses so he could launch his business.

I asked him, "Have you even validated if the market wants this yet?"

He said, "no." I told him to go knock doors and sell the service first. If people buy, then schedule their cleaning for a few days out so he would have time to get the supplies and learn to use them.

Using this validation process, you can prove your business concept before launching. You can test the market to make sure you will be able to sell your product or service at profitable price points. It can also reveal to you key insights to help make your product much better before launching it. If people do not buy it, you can simply ask them, "Why?" Or, "What would I need to change to earn your business?" This can provide key insights into how to improve your offering.

When I wanted to design my first coaching program, I asked a mentor for guidance on how to do it. I was expecting him to tell me to record videos and design course materials. However, he told me the opposite. He told me all I needed for my MVP was a sales pitch to pre-sell with. So, I hosted a workshop and at the end I pitched my new program to the group. Not a single person bought it!

I tweaked my program offer and tried again, and once again no one purchased. Then, I improved my offer and pitched it at a third workshop. This time several people bought it. Pre-selling like this helped me learn exactly what course to build before investing all the time into creating it. Also, this shows the importance of seeking expert counsel. They can save you time, energy, and effort when launching your business.

There are some limitations to this validation method. Unfortunately this method only gives you insights into whether the market is willing to pay for the product or service. It does not necessarily tell you if your product effectively solves the problem. For example, I could have pre-sold my planners with the above email, but people would have hated the design had I never hosted focus groups to validate the quality of the planner first. That is why this strategy will work best when combined with one of the others to validate the product or service quality.

Not all businesses will have this opportunity—some are extremely difficult to presell. You can ask your expert to see if this is appropriate for you.

Validation Questions

Here are some questions to ask your experts:

- How would you recommend I test my business idea in the market?
- How did you test your product or service before launching it? Did you do a soft launch or have people try it out first before doing your official launch?
- How did you determine if there was demand for your product or service before launching it?

Remember, the practices I listed are just the starting point, your expert council is where you will learn the most successful strategies for your industry. Their advice should trump anything I say!

Prepare For Your Expert Counsel

Now that you know the basic process to design and validate your winning product or service, I want to provide additional guidance on how to make the most of your time with your experts.

Even if you think you fully understand your plan without expert counsel, *still* be sure to seek their advice. They may be able to give one piece of advice that saves you thousands of dollars and months of hard work. Plus, having helpful experts to call on in the future when you are faced with challenges or tough decisions will be invaluable, so work to develop those relationships.

Here are some questions to help you identify the unknowns in your business that an expert could help you address:

- What have you spent hours researching that an expert could answer in two minutes?
- What is the biggest unknown for you right now as you get started?
- What are the biggest challenges you're facing that you could ask for advice on?
- What do you need help with?
- What can't you figure out?

Use these to keep growing your list of questions so you are fully prepared for your conversation.

As you are ending your conversation with your expert, additionally ask them, "what questions should I be asking you right now that I haven't?" This might seem like a strange question, but it will help make sure you didn't miss anything vital that you might not have been aware of to ask for.

Lastly, be sure to ask them for referrals of other experts you can meet with.

Bring A Pen And Paper

When you meet your experts, bring a pen and paper. Not an ipad or laptop but actual pen and paper. When someone is speaking to you and you are writing down notes, they feel important. It actually shows that you value the information and will utilize it which makes them want to share more!

Even if you are using a laptop or ipad to take notes, it can come across as rude. Electronics add an element of distraction which can cause your expert to be less helpful. Bring a pen and paper, and take a *lot* of notes.

Also this will be useful for your reference. You might think you will remember everything they say, but you won't. Keep notes.

Reflect And Implement

How will you validate your idea before launching? (beta testers, focus groups, surveys, presales)

_____

_____

_____

_____

What additional questions will you ask your experts?

- What have you spent hours researching that they could answer in two minutes?
- What is the biggest unknown for you right now while getting started?
- What are the biggest challenges you are facing that you could ask for advice with?
- What do you need someone's help with?
- What can't you figure out?

_____

_____

_____

_____

You can download our Validation Plan PDF plus a list of sample questions to ask your experts at **GoalCrazy.com/freedownloads** or by scanning the QR code below:

SCAN ME

CHAPTER 11

THE KNOWLEDGE TRAP

Before we move to the next step in the Goal Crazy Cycle, I need to address one of the big traps I see people fall into way too often during this phase of learning. People get stuck in a cycle of learning tons of knowledge about their business but never taking action. They just keep learning more and more! I call this "The Knowledge Trap."

I had a lady reach out to me once about coaching. She told me that, for the past ten years, she has been working on starting a photography business. She told me that she owned several professional cameras and purchased all the necessary software and equipment to use them. She had taken dozens of courses to learn to use the equipment, shoot pictures, edit them, and even build a website for her business. She had learned a ton!

But guess how many clients she had worked with over that span of ten years? Zero!

She told me she wanted to finish another course on how to grow a business social media page before getting started. I immediately challenged that thought.

I asked her, "If a prospect asked you to take photos for them next week, would you know how to shoot and edit them?"

She replied, "Yes, absolutely!"

I said, "Great—then what you need right now isn't more information; it's action!"

While on the call with her, she made a quick post on her Facebook profile saying, "Hey everyone, I am starting a photography business that specializes in taking high school senior pictures. Do you know anyone who could use my help?"

This was the very first time she had ever marketed her services or even told her friends about this business she had been wanting to start. Within 24 hours, she had people replying to the post and had paying clients within a month.

I know this is an extreme example, but I see variations of this much too often. People get stuck in the learning phase. They typically rationalize this excessive learning with the concept of "knowledge is power." I know this is a popular quote but I want to tell you that it is simply not true. Knowledge is not power. Knowledge is only powerful *if* acted upon.

I want to help you avoid this simple mistake by reviewing several risks that can get you stuck at this phase of the process.

"Knowledge Is Power" Trap

According to the CDC, over 70 percent of Americans are either overweight or obese. Do you think it is lack of knowledge that has led to this? Of course not! We all know it is healthier to be fit and in shape. We also have unlimited knowledge at our fingertips with our smartphones. We can look up meal plans for free, workout routines, and even free workout videos on YouTube to help us.

So, why are so many of us overweight? We are missing *action*, not knowledge.

One time, I met a customer while selling a car who swore to me he had the idea of Facebook before it came out. I am sure we have all met people like this. After he told me that, I asked him, "what did you do with the idea?" He looked at me blankly.

Here's the thing: If knowledge was power, all those people who had the idea of Facebook would be rich right now! But they aren't, because they did nothing with the information. The person who *acted* on it, Mark Zuckerberg, spent years building a website, took massive action, lots of risk, got investors, and now has a giant business (and a freakish amount of power).

Knowledge is not power unless acted upon.

How do you avoid this trap? Set a learning cap. For example, dedicate one month to research, then commit to taking action. I read for 20 minutes a day. I schedule a limited amount of meetings with mentors and coaches per month, because although it is helpful to learn, what I ultimately need to do is put the knowledge into action.

There will be phases in your life when learning is more important. When I first quit my job, I spent several months just interviewing people and taking notes. Maybe you'll need to do something similar. But limit that time! Don't say you'll keep learning until you have complete clarity and certainty—because that will never happen. Set a specific timeframe for learning. Maybe it's 20 minutes per day, one lunch meeting per week, or three months of interviewing others. Whatever it is, set a clear limit and commit to taking action once that time is up.

While knowledge is useful, action is what ultimately moves the needle forward.

People typically fall into this Knowledge Trap out of fear. They are afraid of failure, afraid of the unknown, or afraid of being unprepared. They delay taking action and facing their fears by learning more. If you notice yourself getting stuck in a situation like this, I want you to ask yourself, "Do I truly not know the next step to take, or am I just simply afraid to take it?"

If you know the next step to take and how to take it, then do it! You have all the information you need. If you are unsure what step to take, research more. Remember, no matter how much research you do, you will never gain 100 percent certainty. There will always be a level of risk and fear whenever you need to take an action.

You Can Get Bad Advice

One of the other risks during this phase is potentially getting bad advice. To help reduce the chances of this, make sure you are asking someone who has actually accomplished what you want. I wouldn't ask my landscaper what I should do about a toothache, right?

People often go to friends and family for advice. There is nothing wrong with that in itself. But if your friends and family are not experts in the subject, go ask someone else! If you ask the wrong people, you will get bad advice.

I had a client named Brad who had a business cleaning gutters. He had a pretty simple business model, he would knock on doors and offer a price to clean the person's gutters. He had very few expenses other than gas for his vehicle and a few supplies. Sadly though, he was losing money every month! This is because he was given a bunch of terrible advice from family on how to run a business.

They told Brad to price himself below market value to get sales and then hire several employees to help him grow. He was never told of the many legal responsibilities that accompany W2 employees, such as employment tax and social security. Because Brad was unaware of these, he was actually losing money every hour his employees were working. Eventually, he received a letter from the government that explained he owed them a bunch of money.

I am not trying to say Brad's family was clueless or purposefully trying to ruin his business. They just did not have experience running a business like his. He experienced many large problems that could have easily been avoided if he was given proper advice from the start.

Good advice will make your journey to success quicker and easier. Bad advice will lead to a longer and harder journey. Be selective with the person you ask for guidance from.

People May Say NO

Another risk is that experts will flat out say *no* to your request for help. You might ask someone if they would be willing to let you buy them lunch, or even just to have a 15-minute phone call, and they say, "I don't have time." Don't take it personally, it's okay! That is just part of the process. Go ask someone else. Or ask them who else they know that might be a good person for you to talk to.

Remember, although you might be afraid to ask, there is almost no risk. The worst someone can say is "no." You weren't scheduled to meet with them before you asked, and you won't have a scheduled meeting after they ask, so you are back to where you started. No harm done. However, if you don't ask, you remove all chances of finding help. So, you have the opportunity to benefit and save months of research and trouble, with no risk of harm. Send the text, make the call, and ask!

Often, people are afraid to ask others for help because they think it is a sign of weakness. However, I want to tell you that is not the case. I think most of my mentors are more impressed with the types of questions I ask them than the knowledge I possess. In my experience, most people who have a successful business love to talk about it. If you ask them questions about how they overcame the struggles and made their dream happen they are excited to share. It is their opportunity to glory in the experience. You are providing a service by asking the question and allowing them to help you.

I believe people are born with an innate desire to help others. If someone stops you and asks for directions, oftentimes you feel proud to help them. It is an opportunity for you to show your knowledge and help someone else. The same is true with mentorship. People are excited to share the incredible information and experiences they have accumulated over the years and pass it to someone in need.

Financial Risk

In some cases, you may need to pay for the advice. There can be a financial risk with this step too. I have spent thousands of dollars on coaching over the years. Good mentors and coaches can be expensive!

Just like with any mentor, I always want to double check that the coach I hire has actually accomplished what I want to do. Then I look at reviews of past clients.

Every year, I budget a specific amount of money I want to invest into myself. That is, invest into personal development coaches, conferences, programs, courses, and books throughout the year. I highly recommend you do the same. This investment has paid the best dividends. It is because of these programs that I have learned to start and grow the businesses I have.

Since graduating from college I have invested over $75,000 in personal development programs, coaches, and conferences. That seems like a lot! But it has led to me creating a business portfolio with several million in assets, a life I love, and most importantly, it has formed me into the person I wanted to become. It's worth it!

Now, you don't have to go straight to the big ticket coaching programs. You can start with a $15 book, or a $297 course. But I would be sure to start viewing yourself as an asset worth investing into.

Know It All Risk

One of the biggest mistakes and risks you can take is thinking that you already know it all and avoid asking others for help. Even if these people share information you already know, it's still worth it. You want to build a support team of mentors to turn to when you need it. These people can save you months or years of work when you follow the advice they have learned the hard way.

Too many people want to be "self made" and want to secretly build a big business and only tell people about it once they are successful. A much wiser approach is to ask others for help, and provide help to those who ask it from you.

Reflect And Implement

How long will you dedicate to this "seek expert counsel" phase of your business? Make a plan and set a cap to help you avoid the knowledge trap.

_____

_____

_____

_____

How much are you willing to invest into this expert advice? Maybe you want to invest $40 in buying experts coffee, maybe $500 in courses, or $10,000 in coaching. All are great options! How much will it be for yourself?

_____

_____

_____

_____

CHAPTER 12

STEP TWO—IDENTIFY YOUR MOST IMPACTFUL GOAL

In this next step in the Goal Crazy Cycle, we want to narrow your focus down to the most important elements of your business. After you get advice from your experts, you likely feel overwhelmed with all the aspects of clarifying your target customer, finding their needs, designing a winning product to sell, and validating your idea.

I was reminded of this recently as a client of mine was launching a business selling party supplies online. He felt overwhelmed with all he needed to do for his product launch, especially since this was his first time and he had no clue of how to implement most of the advice his experts had given him. He also had a full-time job, and was exhausted trying to figure out how to fit it all into his already busy life.

I reminded him that the first step was to finalize the design for his product. If he didn't get the product manufactured, nothing else would be relevant because he wouldn't have anything to sell. He set a smaller, 90-day goal to finish his product design so he could place a bulk order with his supplier.

Having a smaller target gave him clarity. He had full confidence he could accomplish it and this allowed him to narrow his focus and get the process started rather than just freaking out at the overwhelm.

After he finished his design, everything else was easier. He started going through the other items on his list and had much more clarity because he then knew exactly what he would be selling.

This reminded me of a silly experience I had as a kid. Growing up, my family lived on a lake and in the summer we would kayak on it. There were six kids in my family and eight of my cousins lived right next door. We had two small kayaks and a bunch of us kids, so we would cram as many people onto each kayak as we could and paddle out into the lake.

I quickly learned there were two ways to make the kayak go faster. One: You could work harder and paddle quicker. Second: You could remove weight, a.k.a. pushing someone off the boat (the preferred method). If you pushed someone off the boat, you would start to go faster without working any harder. You were also much more stable! A kayak with too many people was extremely wobbly and likely to flip. Removing weight was a win-win, unless you were the one pushed off.

These same principles apply when progressing toward your business. I want to compare the kayak to your work day. Just like the kayak, your day cannot fit an unlimited amount of things in it. A kayak has a limited amount of space to fit items and people. Similarly, your day only has 24 hours to fill.

If you want to make progress toward your goals faster, you have two options. First, you can work harder. This is what most people do. If they want to make more progress, they decide to work more hours, or "get busier." Most think this is the only option and often it leads them to working 12+ hour days, seven days a week until the "work harder" option is impossible to keep scaling.

The second option is what most people forget. You can remove weight. Just like the kayak, if you remove items from your day, you can make progress faster on the remaining items without working any harder. Plus it is more enjoyable—just like an over-filled kayak, an over-filled day is frightening, unstable, and likely to end in disaster.

As you start your business, the more you take on at once, the less productive, effective and stable you become. People think multitasking is more efficient, when typically they are slowing themselves down from finishing any single given project.

That is why in this next step, I want to help you narrow your focus down to a 90 day target. You have likely received tons of advice from your expert counsel, so I want to help you sort through it to identify what is most important and then remove the weight of everything else so you can make progress on it quicker. A nice bonus of this process is that it will also help you create the time to actually do the work needed for your business.

Why A 90 Day Target?

Over the years of coaching people, I have found 90 days to be the ideal time frame on which to focus on. 90 days gives you enough time to take massive actions and make big shifts. But it is short enough that the end is in sight, and therefore gives you the motivation to push through to make deadlines happen. Even though it will likely take you longer than 90 days to start your business, I want you to break it down into a 90 day milestone to aim at that will move you in the direction of getting your business started. At the end of the 90 days, you can reflect on your progress and set a new goal for the next 90 days. Keep repeating this process until your business is launched.

How To Identify Your 90 Day Goal

In one of my favorite books, *The One Thing,* Gary Keller asks the question, "What is the one thing I can do such that by doing it everything else will be easier or irrelevant?"

This is such a powerful question and one that has helped me make progress toward my goals quickly. I want you to ask yourself something similar. With your dream business in mind, ask yourself, "What is the one thing I can do in the next 90 days for my business that would make everything else easier or irrelevant?"

You want to find a 90 day goal that is realistic. You want it to be an activity that will push your comfort zone, but still be within the capabilities of what you believe you can accomplish. This will give you motivation to get started.

We will call this 90 day goal your "Most Impactful Goal," because I want you to clearly see it is the most important thing to focus on with your business. It is too easy to get distracted with all the demands of your business. If you don't have a priority goal, you will be spread too thin and make little progress. Obviously you can accomplish more than just this one thing, but you must identify what will be your main objective. You can still have smaller supportive tasks and projects during those 90 days, but it is key that you have this one dominating Most Impactful Goal that will take priority over everything else.

It is important to have this 90 day target be an *action*-based goal rather than a *results*-based goal. An action-based goal is a target you set for yourself of the type of actions you want to complete. An example of an action-based goal would be to ask ten experts to lunch, make 50 social media posts about your business, make 100 sales calls, or dedicate 100 hours to working on your business. All of these are based on actions you can take. You have complete control over whether you perform the actions or not.

Result-based goals are results you want to get from the actions you take. Examples could be $100k in sales, $10,000 per month in profit, or being top ranked for your business keywords.

In Chapter Six we created visions for yourself. Those were result-based. They are the results you are wanting to achieve based on the actions you will take with your new business. Although they are important, you do not always have complete control over whether these goals are achieved or not because they are reliant on other factors than yourself. However, your action-based goals should move you in the direction of your results-based goals. For example, you do not always have complete control over whether you hit your desired result of generating $10,000 in profit. However, you do have control over whether you hit your action-based goal, such as making 100 prospecting calls. Making those prospecting calls should lead to hitting your profit goal.

For this first round going through the Goal Crazy Cycle, the focus should be on designing and validating your product or service. Based on your conversations with your experts, can you create your winning product and service over the next 90 days? If so, great! That will be your Most Impactful Goal. If not, clarify a milestone you can take toward it. Such as, order a prototype, get several samples, host three focus groups etc.

What will your Most Impactful Goal be for this quarter? What is the one thing you can do this quarter for your business that will make everything else easier or irrelevant?

The Biggest Obstacle

There is one unavoidable obstacle I must still address, because it will try to stop you from achieving your Most Impactful Goal. There is an obstacle that we all face that has stopped most people from ever accomplishing their dreams. That obstacle is distraction.

Distraction is the largest obstacle in the way of you accomplishing your goals and dreams. The whole world has an agenda of what it wants you to do with your time and attention and is constantly fighting to try and capture it. Everyone wants you to focus on their ads, their software, their news articles, etc. They will distract you from ever getting ahead!

These distractions can be small things like email notifications or phone calls, but also they can be bigger things, such as your other goals. As we discussed earlier, often your other goals become obstacles in the way of accomplishing your Most Impactful Goal. All the small tasks and projects involved with starting your business can distract you from achieving your primary, heavy-hitting target of creating your winning product/service.

A few weeks ago a salesman cold called me trying to sell me marketing software that he claimed would grow my online business.

He asked, "Jason, would you like your sales to increase?"

I responded, "No."

He asked, "Well, don't you want to earn more profits?"

I once again responded, "No."

He was confused.

I explained, "Even if your software worked perfectly and skyrocketed my business I still wouldn't want it. Right now, I am working on writing a book, and if I say yes to growing my online store, I will be saying no to my book by default."

If you are serious about making your business happen, and I imagine you are since you have made it this far into the book, then you need to create boundaries like this for your own Most Impactful Goal too!

You will face many small and large distractions that try to stop you from pursuing your dream business. Maybe you wake up early to work on your Most Impactful Goal, but then check your email and spend the next 30 minutes replying to requests from coworkers. Maybe you block off an evening to work your plan, but then decide to play the TV in the background while you eat dinner and suddenly your entire evening is gone. It can happen so easily!

It is important to remember that, when you say "yes" to one thing, you are inevitably saying "no" to something else. For example, if you say yes to getting together with friends tonight, you say no to having a quiet night with your family.

Unfortunately, people start to say yes to many meaningless small activities and tasks, which ultimately makes them say no to their bigger goals. They say yes to scrolling social media, so therefore say no to taking actions for their business. They say yes to their snooze button, and say no to intentionally planning their day.

So, how do we avoid these distractions? Luckily, this step in the Goal Crazy Method really has two parts. The first is clarifying what your Most Impactful Goal will be for the next 90 days. Then the second step is clarifying the potential distractions and creating a plan to avoid them. Basically we make a plan to *protect* your time so that you have the space in your calendar to make your Most Impactful Goal happen.

Protect Your Time

People often tell me that they "need more time." Unfortunately, it is impossible to get more time! You only get 24 hours per day, you cannot get more, you cannot have less. So, rather than focusing on gaining more time, you need to focus on protecting the time you have for what is most important.

Since you have already clarified your Most Impactful Goal, we need to clarify all the other projects, tasks, and distractions that can get in the way of you making it happen. We need to create a No/Not Now List.

I will help you form a list of all the things you must say no or not now to this quarter so that you can ultimately say yes to your Most Impactful Goal.

I often have business owners sign me on as their coach because they want to accomplish *more*. The ironic thing is that I help them accomplish less! It sounds counterintuitive, but the key is that I help them accomplish the right things, so they are able to make more progress and get better results without needing to work harder. That is what this Most Impactful Goal will help you do in your own life. Now that you have clarified yours, you will have the freedom to say no (or not now) to the activities getting in the way of it.

Reflect on which projects, tasks, and commitments you will say no or not now to this quarter so that you can have time to accomplish your Most Impactful Goal. What potential distractions could get in the way?

Remember, these might be activities that are related to your business but aren't directly related to your Most Impactful Goal. For example, when I was designing my planner, one of the biggest distractions was creating my website. Even though the website was important, it would be completely irrelevant if I never had a planner finished. I needed to say no to designing my website, until my planner design was finished.

These also could be activities in your personal life, such as saying no to your pool league for the quarter while you get your business started.

Remember, just because you will say no to something now, that doesn't mean you can never do it. It means you just will wait until later in the future. So, take time now to clarify your No/Not Now List for this coming quarter.

Guardrails

After you clarify the projects that might distract you, make a strategy to prevent yourself from accidentally falling into them. We need to create guardrails so that these distractions don't sneak in. Just like you have guardrails on the side of the road to protect yourself from danger, you need guardrails to protect you from these distractions.

Although we all have great intentions of getting focused, we often default to what is most convenient. For example, if the laptop you work on is kept upstairs and your TV remote is within arm's length, you will likely reach for the remote even if you had every intention of going upstairs to work, simply because the TV remote is closer. It is all too easy to choose what is most convenient.

We need to flip this around.

If your TV is what distracts you, put the remote in a room far away. Put it upstairs in your closet and put your laptop on your dining room table where it's easy to access. If your house has many little projects that distract you from getting work done, go to a coffee shop and work there. Remove yourself from the distractions.

Reflecting on your own life, consider how you can make working on your goals more convenient. Additionally, how can you make your distractions less convenient? How can you put up barriers that block you from your distractions?

Reflect And Implement

What will be your Most Impactful Goal this quarter?

- What is the one thing you can do this quarter for your business that will make everything else easier or irrelevant?

_____

_____

_____

_____

What will be on your No/Not Now List for the quarter:

- What will you say no or "not now" to so you can make your Most Impactful Goal happen?
- What other potential distractions that can get in the way of your goal?

_____

_____

_____

_____

What are some guardrails you can put in place to protect yourself from falling off course?

- How can you make working on your goals more convenient?
- How can you remove yourself from the environment of distractions?
- How can you make distractions less convenient to keep yourself from falling into them?

_____

_____

_____

_____

Download a free PDF of this exercise along with our Most Impactful Goal Planning sheets that help you create clear plans to accomplish your goals. These sheets are taken directly from our Goal Crazy Planner, and you can access them free at our website: **GoalCrazy.com/freedownloads** or by scanning the QR code below:

CHAPTER 13

STEP THREE—TAKE MESSY ACTION

As I mentioned in a prior chapter, when I first wanted to buy rental properties, I called a past customer I had sold a car to to ask for advice. He told me that I should start touring properties.

At first I didn't like this advice. I wasn't sure how to analyze a deal, find tenants, get financing, and I still needed a few more months to save up the money to buy one.

It seemed silly to tour a property when I was still so new to the process. But, even though I didn't feel ready at all, I followed his advice and started calling real estate agents to schedule tours. At first, I had no clue what I was looking at. I couldn't have recognized a good deal if it slapped me in the face. I walked through each property and asked the real estate agent *tons* of questions about what I should be looking at. I slowly learned red flags to watch for and valuable qualities to seek out in a property. I toured properties with issues, and started researching what various repairs would cost to fix. I started gathering numbers for each property and analyzed the returns I expected to generate. Then, the real estate agent connected me with lenders to learn how to finance a property when I found the right one.

Without realizing it, I was given the confidence to pull the trigger and buy my first property. I had learned to analyze deals, recognize an attractive one, and get it financed. One of the biggest lessons from this experience was how I learned *way* more from going out and taking action than I would have if I simply read books and watched real estate videos.

I tell this story because I really want to show the power of action. Action brings clarity. Once you start taking action, the next steps get clearer. I also want you to realize that you *must* take action before you feel ready. Often, people wait until they have clarity to take action, when in reality, the action is what will bring the clarity in the first place.

As you are starting your business you must take *messy* action. Messy action is the next step in the Goal Crazy Cycle. You need to take actions that aren't 100 percent clear, where you risk making mistakes. You must take action before you know what you are doing.

When our daughter is learning to walk, she takes tons of messy action. She tries to walk, run, and jump before she is ready. She falls again and again. That is a messy action! This is what it looks like to grow. Just imagine if a child wanted to wait until they fully understood how to walk before walking. They would never move. They need to simply get started even though they have no clue what they are doing. It's how they learn.

The reality is, you will *never* feel completely ready to act. You will never have 100 percent certainty on anything, so if you wait for certainty and complete clarity you will spend your entire life waiting. Clarity comes from action, not the other way around. If you are unsure of the path to accomplish your goals, just ask yourself, "What is the next indicated step?"

Once you take that step, the next one will present itself.

I don't want to discredit the importance of learning and research. Often the next indicated step is to research. But remember, there are only two pieces of information you need to take action—a clear goal and an indicated step toward that goal. That's it! If you have both of those items, you have all you need to start taking action. Often people get stuck trying to clarify the entire plan before starting when they already know plenty of actions they can take right now that would move them closer to their goal.

What Is Your Next Step

Looking over the advice you received from your expert counsel and at your 90 day target, what is the next indicated step to take toward it?

As simple as it might sound, starting a business is simply an investment of time. Ask yourself, "How much time have I invested into my business? How many hours of actual work have I put into it?"

For most people, this is *zero* hours. If that's the case, get started! You will need to take actions, learn from them, get advice about the actions you took, redo some of the actions, then take new actions. Luckily, once you start the process, the next step will keep presenting itself. What can you do today for 20 minutes that will move you closer to your goal? Then look to see what opportunities present themselves as you take those actions.

Find A Way To Commit

People often get stuck on this step. They learn the actions they need to take, make a plan to accomplish them, but don't follow through. I want to give you additional help so that you *will* take action. You need to find a way to commit. How can you hold yourself accountable?

I will show you two approaches to accountability. The first will teach you how to use others to hold yourself accountable, and the second will teach you ways of holding yourself accountable.

Accountability From Others

One of the best ways to follow through on your plan is to find a person you can be held accountable to. At first, you might not have anyone, so I want to give you a couple examples of ways you can create accountability so you can learn how to do this for yourself.

I was teaching a group course a few years ago and one of the participants told me how he wanted to start a side business detailing cars. He already had half of the equipment needed and a few friends had been asking him to detail their cars. But, for the past two years, he had been trying to "figure the rest out" before starting. He still needed to figure out how much to charge, how to accept payment, and what supplies to buy.

I told him, "Call one of your friends today and schedule a detail for them in two weeks. That way you have a deadline of two weeks to 'figure out the rest.' More importantly, now you *have* to figure it out so you can deliver on the detail you scheduled for your friend's car!"

Turns out, once he created this deadline for himself he realized he was only a few quick decisions away from having his side business running. Now he has a detailing business, just because of that first customer. All he needed was a little accountability to finally get started.

For your goal, try and find how you can commit to someone else to deliver. If you want to start networking, maybe you can invite a friend to register for an event with you. Now you *have* to show up or you will let your friend down. Maybe you can pre-sell your product or service, now you *have* to deliver on it. If you want to start buying real estate, ask a friend to tour some properties with you next weekend. Now you have to call real estate agents and schedule tours.

When I was working on designing my planner, I needed help holding myself accountable to create the design, so I reached out to a mentor or mine and said:

Hey _____, I have been working on designing a planner that will help people accomplish their goals. Your advice and guidance would be extremely helpful since I know you are a high achiever yourself. Would you be free to meet sometime next week to look over the design with me? I am relatively free on Tuesday or Thursday if you have any availability then.

The funny thing is that when I called this mentor, I had not even started my planner design yet. But once I scheduled the meeting I *had* to finish it. I created for myself accountability to someone else to get the design made.

Now, I want you to think about your own goals. How can you make a commitment to someone else to deliver on your actions? How can you get someone else involved? Schedule a meeting with them to report on an action that you need to be held accountable to do. If you are working on designing your MVP, schedule a meeting with a beta tester or expert to show it to them. This will force you to make your MVP by that date.

Accountability To Yourself

Although people are generally more likely to follow through on accountability from others, learning to hold yourself accountable is still a very powerful skill. I want to go over a few tools that are really helpful to make this happen.

Deadlines

Once you have your goal, list out the action steps needed to accomplish the goal and give yourself a deadline for each activity. By each activity, write the date by which you will accomplish it. Deadlines are powerful tools as long as you treat them seriously. Think back to school—if a teacher gave you a deadline you would find a way to fulfill it, even if it meant staying up all night to finish the project. Use this power for your advantage!

If you really want to add some incentive, decide on a reward you will give yourself if you hit the deadline. Maybe you can get yourself a fancy meal or treat yourself to something else you've wanted.

To make this step extra powerful, combine it with the previous strategy and share your deadline with someone else. You will be more likely to fulfill commitments to someone else than to just yourself.

Score Card

One technique we use in the Goal Crazy Planner is a score card. The basic concept is to plan out a template of your ideal day, then grade yourself each night on how close you came to that ideal.

In the Goal Crazy Planner, we call this our Habit Card. However, it is easy to make your own even without our planner.

Here is an example of items I have on the score card for myself right now:

- Get up on my first alarm
- Workout for 20 minutes
- Accomplish my number one goal for the day
- Give my wife a break from watching the kids
- Work on my book for at least an hour
- Be in bed by 9:30 p.m.

I have these items listed on a small card, and each night I review this same list to grade myself on how close I came to my ideal.

People often think it is impossible to live their ideal life, when all it comes down to is defining what their ideal day would be, then working to live it out one day at a time. A score card will help you do exactly that!

Reflect right now for yourself:

- What would your ideal day look like?.
- What would your morning look like?
- What tasks would you complete throughout the day?
- What would your evening include?

Make yourself your own scorecard and then put it on your nightstand so you can easily review it each night to see how close you came.

We have included as part of this book a free training on how to create your own scorecard for yourself. You can access this training at **GoalCrazy. com/freedownloads**

Your Plans Will Change

A final tip before we continue on in the process: Know in advance that, once you start taking action toward your goals, your plans will likely change. This is normal! It is part of the process.

About three years ago I launched the Goal Crazy Podcast. Ironically, it happened accidentally. I had always dreamed of starting a podcast, but I thought it would be much further out in the future. I had wanted to find a fun way to make content for my business and connect with other entrepreneurs.

Originally, I thought it would be fun to interview business owners about their entrepreneurial journeys and post the recordings on my blog for Goal Crazy. I set a goal to do one interview that month and see how it went. I figured most business owners would be too busy to do something like this, so I emailed five entrepreneurs asking if I could interview them hoping at least one would say yes. Surprisingly, all five said yes! So, I changed my goal from doing one interview, to recording five.

At the end of my first interview, the guest asked me the name of my podcast. I told her, "I'm sorry there must have been a miscommunication. I don't have a podcast. This is just going on my blog and will then be sent out to my email list."

She looked at me with sincere encouragement and said, "Jason, you should really think about starting a podcast, I think you have a talent for it!"

The craziest thing happened next—all four of the other people I interviewed told me the same thing! One gentleman was so convinced of it that after our recording he shared the basics of how he started his own podcast and sent me his editor's contact details.

After a quick call to the editor, I decided to change my 90 day goal again, this time to launching a podcast rather than making blog posts.

I tell you all of this because it is a good illustration of how action brings clarity and how your plans will likely change.

Earlier, I talked about the importance of a 90 day goal. Every quarter I set a Most Impactful Goal for the quarter and make a basic plan to accomplish it. Very frequently, my plan to accomplish the goals, and sometimes even the goal itself, changes as I get started working toward it. As ironic as it sounds, it is a good thing!

Once I start taking action, I get more clarity and see a new plan that will not only get me to the original goal, but it will exceed it. Then I shift direction toward that new goal and I get clarity again as I take action.

See the picture below of how my goal had changed from interviewing one guest for my blog to launching a podcast.

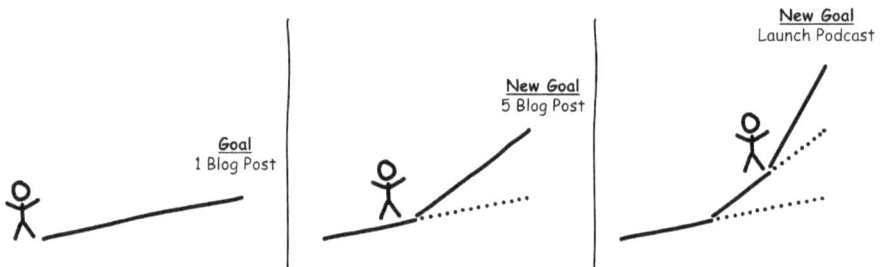

Things don't always happen this way. There have been plenty of times when I worked the plan pretty close to what I originally laid out. However, it normally changes for the better once I get started.

When we set our goals and make our initial plans, we have limited information. But once we take action, we get more information and better clarity. Because of this, our plans and goals often shift. The purpose of the goal is to give you clarity and draw you into action. As long as it is doing that, it is working!

I will warn you though, if you keep jumping from one goal to a completely different goal, you will never make progress. I only adjust my goal if I see a new opportunity to reach my dream faster. For example, my podcast provided the opportunity to create content and share it with my audience, just as the blog was intended to. In this instance, the podcast would provide an opportunity to reach this desired outcome in a more efficient and enjoyable manner.

Compare this to recording the first interview and then deciding to change my goal to buying another rental property. That would have been completely changing directions from the original intention and would make progress impossible. When you make adjustments toward your goals and plans, make sure the changes are still moving you in the overall direction of the original goal.

Reflect And Implement

Look over your goal and the advice you received from others, and clarify the next indicated step to take.

- What could you do for 20 minutes that would move you closer to your goal?
- What is the next indicated step for you to act on?

_____

_____

_____

_____

Accountability

- By when will you accomplish this action step?
- How will you hold yourself accountable?
- How can you make a commitment to someone else to take this action?
- How will you make a commitment to yourself to take action?

_____

_____

_____

_____

How have your plans changed as a result of taking action? What new opportunities have presented themselves?

_____

_____

_____

_____

Before you move onto the next section, set a timer for 20 minutes to start working on your goal. Even if it is simply spent filling out the PDF, researching, or making a phone call. Dedicate 20 minutes today to move yourself a little closer toward your Most Impactful Goal.

If you need extra help holding yourself accountable, check out our accountability programs at GoalCrazy.com/programs

Additionally, access the accompanying PDF to help you clarify this action and make a scorecard to hold you accountable to achieve it. Find this training at **GoalCrazy.com/freedownloads** or by scanning the QR code below:

SCAN ME

CHAPTER 14

THIS IS WHAT GROWTH FEELS LIKE

Now that we have clarified your goals and the next steps to take, are you likely feeling nervous about actually getting started?

Often what keeps people from ever taking action toward their business is that it opens up the potential of risk. When faced with risk, it is natural to start to feel anxious and even afraid. This is a natural part of growth. Before we go any further into the Goal Crazy Cycle, I want to address the risks of taking action and the feelings of anxiety that come with it so you can push past this hurdle. If you allow fear to prevent you from taking action, you will never get your business started.

Now, I realize taking risks is frightening. One of my past clients, Mike, started a martial arts school. Before he started it, he was extremely nervous about running a business. He knew the martial arts practice well, but the idea of leasing a building, getting clients, keeping the books, and hiring employees seemed terrifying. He had no business experience so entrepreneurship was *way* outside his comfort zone.

After a few years of running his business, all the behind the scenes "business stuff" that he was so worried about–like bookkeeping, payroll, marketing, insurance etc, required very little of his attention. He's able to run those aspects of the business without thinking much about it. He has now gotten so comfortable with it that he has been able to go after much bigger goals like opening several more martial art schools.

This is what I want to help you do with your business. I want to help give you the confidence to push your comfort zone and accomplish your ambitious goals. That way, in the future you will have the mental strength to go after even bigger ones. It will be extremely rewarding to create the life you have dreamed of, but what will be even more valuable is the confidence you gain in yourself. You will be able to go after targets much farther outside your comfort zone and trust you can find a way to make them happen.

Risk And Growth

When I say risk, I'm not talking about going and buying a lottery ticket, gambling at the casino, or engaging in reckless behavior. Those are unhealthy risks. I am talking about healthy risks, like betting on yourself, pushing yourself to take new actions and stepping into the unknown. You can't keep doing the same things you always have done and expect growth to happen. You need to learn something new, do something new, meet someone new, or think something new.

Whenever you do something new however, there is a risk. Since you have never done it before, the outcome is unknown to you. But if you think back in your life, you will see that all of your current capabilities have come when you have stepped out of your comfort zone and taken a risk, whether big or small. When you take risks, you increase your capabilities.

This isn't just true for business, it applies to all areas of life. When you want a relationship, you need to risk being rejected. When you want to get in shape, you need to risk the insecurity of going to the gym even when you are embarrassed about your appearance and ability. When you want to learn a new skill, you must risk being a beginner. If you want to start a business, you must risk failing. And if you want your business to grow, you will need to keep taking risks to increase your entrepreneurial capabilities.

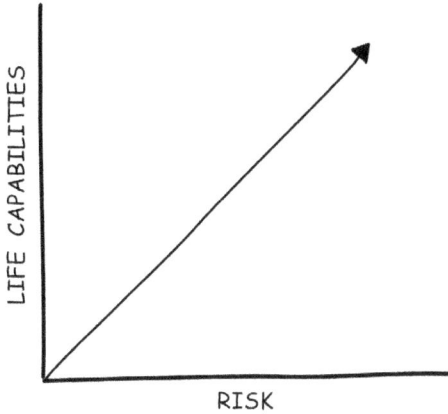

Let me show you how this concept applies to the entrepreneur I mentioned earlier, Mike. For him to learn how to run his own school, he needed to risk failing at it. When he wanted to learn to market his business and grow it, he had to risk losing money on marketing campaigns that didn't work. When he wanted to hire an employee, he needed to risk giving someone else a portion of the revenue, and risk that the employee might not be a good fit. When he wanted to open another location for his business, he had to risk that location failing. However, with each risk he took, he learned a new skill. By taking risks he learned to start a business, market it, hire employees, and even open a second location.

Unfortunately, most people avoid taking risks. Once they get to a level where they feel comfortable they stop pushing themselves. Often this happens once a person gets a job that supports their lifestyle. They get content and stop taking risks or learning more. Obviously it is okay to stop taking risks if you are happy with the status of your life. But if you are unhappy where you are, then you need to start taking risks again to get somewhere else. Taking risks will be required in order to learn the skills necessary to launch a successful business.

Anxiety Will Come

When you take a risk, you will experience anxiety. It is our body's natural way of dealing with it. The nature of risk is that there is a level of uncertainty, and when we experience uncertainty our body creates anxiety. If there wasn't uncertainty, there wouldn't be risk.

At first this anxiety might seem like a bad thing because it's uncomfortable. But I want you to retrain your mindset to see that as a good thing. People have this misconception that all anxiety and discomfort are bad, when in fact, they are not. They serve an important purpose.

Dr. David Rosmarin, an associate professor at Harvard Medical School, has done a lot of research around the benefits of anxiety and how it is part of growth. In one of his talks, he gives an analogy I love. He explains, if you want to get stronger, you go to the gym and lift weights. If you have done this, you know it's a painful process. You lift the weights and your arms start to burn. Now imagine if you were trying to strictly avoid all discomfort while working out. It would be impossible, right? If you avoided this pain and stopped working out, you'd prevent yourself from ever getting stronger. However, if you push past the pain, continue working out, and allow your muscles to grow, you will be able to lift the same weights with less discomfort.

Dr. Rosmarin said our anxiety works just the same. When we engage in a new activity our body releases anxiety. It is just part of the process. It might help to think of your brain as a mental muscle, and when you start taking new actions and challenges it releases anxiety as part of the process of growing. Similar to your muscles, as you start to engage in the new actions more, things will get easier, and will eventually stop causing the uncomfortable feelings.

Accept that anxiety and discomfort will accompany you as you start to grow your business. It's a good thing. It means you are growing. Obviously if you have an uncontrollable or unmanageable amount of anxiety, seek professional help, but normal amounts of anxiety are expected.

I think too many people try to avoid anxiety and discomfort at all costs. Often when I am working with clients they will share, "That makes me feel anxious," or, "That makes me uncomfortable," and I respond *"Good!"*

I have never once met a successful entrepreneur who told me that they became successful by avoiding everything that made them anxious or uncomfortable. Typically it is the exact opposite! They intentionally sought out opportunities that made them incredibly uncomfortable and anxious and pushed through. That's what led them to grow and expand their comfort zone so that they could handle bigger and bigger challenges.

When you experience anxiety, fear, overwhelm, stress, and challenge on this journey, just remind yourself, "This is what growth feels like." Observe how it feels in your body, notice how your heart rate increases, your breathing speeds up, and blood travels to your arms and legs. This is your body's natural response to prepare for the new challenge in front of you. Don't freak out or be surprised by it, be grateful for it. It means you are growing.

I want to give you a few tools to help manage these feelings.

One of the main tools is journaling. Journaling is a proven tool to help people reduce stress, anxiety, and overwhelm. I take time each morning and evening to journal my thoughts. This provides me a way to process my thoughts, and take them out of my head by writing them on paper. That way my fears and worries are not running wild throughout my head influencing my decisions and actions. We will talk more about specific techniques for this later in the book.

I also find it helpful to talk with mentors and other entrepreneurs about my concerns. Experts can give me good advice on ways to mitigate risks and even point out when they are unnecessary.

Probably the biggest tool is patience. Realize that anxiety is just part of the process the first time you do anything. With time, anxiety and fears will naturally reduce as you get comfortable taking new types of actions. Our goal is to grow the amount of problems, situations, and experiences you can handle by slowly stepping further and further outside of your comfort zone.

It Takes Discipline

Since there are fears around taking action, it will feel easier to do nothing. Discipline is required in these moments.

I think people have a misconception about what discipline means and how it applies to their goals. Many people believe discipline is the willpower to do things they do *not* want to do, when I believe it is exactly the opposite. I view discipline as having the willpower to do what you *want*. For example, I *want* to get up on my first alarm, I *want* to take actions that push my comfort zone, I *want* to live a healthy lifestyle. Oftentimes I don't feel like it, but I want to do it.

One of my greatest desires is for you to create the habit of doing what you *want* in life rather than just what feels comfortable. Not just in big instances like pursuing your dream business rather than settling for the job you hate, but in small instances too, like ordering a side salad rather than french fries. Give yourself permission to do what you truly desire!

Starting a business is an opportunity to allow your dreams to reform you in a substantially healthy way. Rather than being a slave to comfort or to what is easy and feels good, break free and do what you want. Regardless of whether you feel like it, find the willpower to take action anyway. The more you do this, the easier it will get.

The Worst Risk Of All

I know accepting the risks of taking action is scary. However, the results of not taking any risk are even scarier. If you stop taking risks, you guarantee for yourself an average life. As ironic as it sounds, "playing it safe" is the riskiest thing you can do! One of my friends, Dan DeMatte, says in his book *Dream Bigger,* "He who risks nothing great in his life, risks doing nothing great with his life." If you refuse to take a risk, you refuse the life you desire. You destine yourself for mediocrity when you were born for greatness.

The worst risk you can take is waiting until tomorrow to get started on your dream business. There are more people that have said, "I'll wait until the timing is better," and spent the rest of their lives in mediocrity, than there are people who pursued their dreams and failed.

Obviously I do not want you to take reckless risks in your business. We want to reduce the chance of failure as much as possible, and the best way to do that is to speak to experts in your industry as mentioned in Chapter 8. You can learn from their mistakes and get advice for action steps proven to be successful for them. Once you have been given the guidance from your experts on what actions to take, it ultimately falls on you to accept the risks and take action.

Success comes from action, and failure comes from inaction. It is that simple.

Reflect And Implement

Acknowledge how you are feeling at this point in the process. What fears do you have around starting your business?

_____

_____

_____

_____

Remind yourself, this is what growth feels like! Seek expert guidance to reduce the risks, then take action based on their proven strategies.

What are some of the action steps you know could be helpful, but have shied away from because of fear? By when will you commit to taking these actions?

_____

_____

_____

_____

If you are experiencing fears and limiting beliefs that are presenting you from taking action, access our bonus mindset training for free at **GoalCrazy.com/freedownloads** or by scanning the QR code below:

CHAPTER 15

STEP FOUR—REFLECTION

I play golf occasionally. I don't play it much, so I am fairly bad at it. If I were to go out to the driving range and hit 100 golf balls, maybe ten of them would be decent hits, while the other 90 would be terrible.

With that in mind, if I started going to the driving range every day to practice would I get better or worse? I *should* get better, right? But why?

People say practice makes perfect. Technically, I would be practicing my bad swings more than my good ones! I would practice swinging the club wrong 90 times and only practice hitting it well ten times. Wouldn't that make me worse?

As you surely know, this isn't the case. If I were to practice regularly, the number of bad swings would gradually decrease, and the number of good swings would increase. Why is that? It's because of this wonderful thing called reflection. After each swing I reflect on the hit and make mental notes that help me improve. I reflect on how the swing went compared to how I wanted it to go. If I didn't reflect, then I would get more consistent at my bad swings since I had done more of them. Reflection leads to growth.

That brings me to our next step in this process. By reflecting you can make adjustments, learn lessons, and identify the next appropriate action to take, so you don't get worse as a result of the actions, but better.

When you first hear me say reflection, you might think this is an optional step. I want to tell you this step will make more of an impact on your life than any other if done properly! The other steps will not be productive without a strong commitment to this one.

I have met tons of entrepreneurs with big goals, who take massive action, but seem to stay in a place of struggle indefinitely. Why? Because they are missing this step! Twice a day I take time for reflection. I also take longer periods at the end of each week, month, quarter, and year.

You need dedicated time to step away from the business to work *on* it rather than *in* it. More importantly, you need to step away from the business to work on yourself, because when you improve yourself the business will naturally follow. Ironically as it sounds, taking time away from your work to reflect will make you much more productive.

Increase Productivity

By committing to do a deep reflection on your life every 90 days, you will quickly realize you can accomplish four times more in a year than most people. Most people only think about their goals (or the direction of their lives) once a year, usually in January. At the start of the year, people reflect on what they accomplished and set goals for what they want to tackle in the year to come.

The problem is that, after they set their goals on January 1st, they think to themselves, "I have all year! I don't need to get started on these goals right away." Maybe they take a few action steps, but don't have urgency to complete anything. Before they know it, summer arrives, and they are busy with trips, weddings, and family parties, so they "don't have time" to dedicate toward their goals. Then the fall comes and they say, "Well the year is almost over, I'll get started next year." They finish out the small project and then push off the big goals until next year.

Have you ever fallen into this trap? It's sad, and keeps you from getting the results you truly want.

You can avoid this if you reflect on your goals at least quarterly (every 90 days). If your first quarter was bad, that's okay. You can adjust and get back on track for the second quarter. This is much better than waiting until next year! However, if you had a great first quarter, that's wonderful too. You can keep the momentum going and start your second quarter out with confidence.

Now, although reflection is just one step in this process, I want to elaborate on this step from several different angles.

Accomplishments

One of the most important things to reflect on is your accomplishments. So often entrepreneurs think only about the things they have *not* done rather than the things they *have*. This brings them down, making them feel behind and overwhelmed.

Instead, I want you to take time to reflect on what you *have* accomplished. This will boost your confidence to go out and accomplish more. I take time to write out my accomplishments at the end of every day, week, month, quarter, and year. Over the years I have filled dozens of notebooks with accomplishments ranging from small tasks to large impactful goals. I have shelves on my bookshelf full of these journals. I know it might sound silly, but it boosts my confidence!

Whenever I set a new goal, I have a visual reminder and proof of all the things I have accomplished right in front of me. I have thousands of documented accomplishments that give me a strong foundation to go out and accomplish more. By taking time to reflect on my accomplishments I start to identify myself as an accomplisher because I regularly see the goals I've written being accomplished. It convinces me that I'm an *accomplisher* rather than just someone who is *accomplished.*

Someone who is accomplished has made achievements in the past but is still insecure about making achievements in the future. Someone who is an accomplisher is secure in their capabilities of achieving targets both in the past and in the future.

Now, I am not mentioning my accomplishments to brag, I am sure you have thousands of them too. If you are like most though, you just don't think about them. Rather, your mind reminds you of all the things you failed to do. This reduces your confidence when you want to start a new goal, because your thoughts dwell on the goals you failed to accomplish, making it pointless to try again.

I want to change that. At the end of this chapter, I will share an exercise to help you reflect on your accomplishments and to build your confidence. Also, if you really want help forming this habit and rewiring your thinking to that of an accomplisher, the Goal Crazy Planner has built-in reflections that help. You can download a free sample of the planner at GoalCrazy. com/freedownloads.

An easy way to implement this is by taking two minutes each night to write out all you've accomplished over the course of the day. Write down the big accomplishments and the small. You'll start to impress yourself. Oftentimes entrepreneurs get to the end of the day and feel like the whole day escaped them with no clue where the time went. These exercises will help you recognize where it went. Even if you didn't accomplish your original plan, you will still give yourself credit for all the other tasks you did instead.

Mistakes

Another key area to reflect on is our mistakes. I learned the importance of mistakes early on in life.

Growing up, my family water skied in the summers. Whenever I wanted to learn a new trick, I knew that falling was part of the learning process. I fell dozens of times until I finally landed the trick and started to get consistent.

Eventually, I realized the skier who was the best was *not* the person who had fallen the least in their skiing career. The opposite was true. They were the ones who fell the most! They had fallen hundreds of times on their way to learning incredible tricks and becoming great.

I think this concept is true for much of life. To learn, you must make mistakes. Unfortunately we view mistakes as a final destination. We view ourselves like the man in the graphic below who is either moving toward success or failure. If we make a mistake, we believe we are on the path to failure. If we perform correctly we are on the path to success. Can you relate to this?

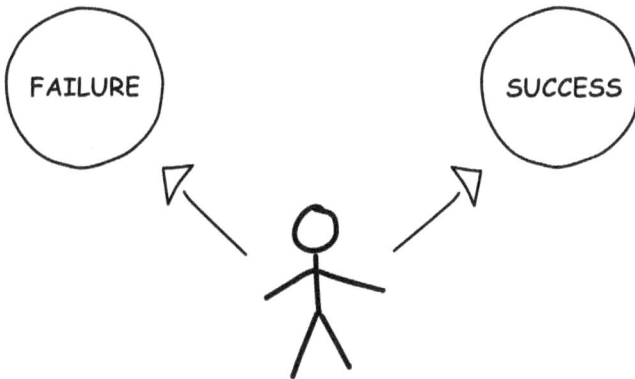

However, I have found something different to be true! First you need to fail, *then* you can succeed. Failure is a key part of entrepreneurship.

A few months ago I had an inspiring entrepreneur named Matt Raad on my podcast to share his entrepreneurial journey. Matt began when he found a business for sale that he was passionate about. Speaking with his accountant and looking at the business for himself, it seemed like a great buy. Unfortunately after he purchased the business, he realized there were areas of the business that had been neglected for years putting the whole organization on track for bankruptcy.

Rather than viewing his new business as a failure, he worked ruthlessly to make it a success. Not only did he save the business, but he created processes so that the business only required a few hours per week to run.

The most beneficial part was that it taught Matt an extremely valuable skillset. He learned to identify poorly performing businesses which he could buy for cheap, and then optimize them to meet their potential. With those skills, he bought dozens more businesses.

Not only has Matt built a portfolio of successful businesses, but he also teaches courses helping other entrepreneurs learn how to do the same thing. All of this started from his first business, which was on the edge of bankruptcy, and could have easily been viewed as a mistake.

I want you to know that mistakes and challenges are not *in the way* of you becoming a great entrepreneur. They *are the way* to become a great entrepreneur. This is simply what growth looks like. Not getting it right the first time doesn't mean you are a failure, it means you are an entrepreneur.

I can tell you that I have made hundreds of mistakes, spent hours on projects that failed, lost thousands of dollars on bad advertising campaigns, and embarrassed myself more times than I can count. But when I reflect, it is so clear to see how necessary all of these mistakes were to the formation of myself today. Think back to the story of my first focus group for my planner and receiving terrible feedback. I wanted to quit! I felt defeated.

You will have times when you are faced with a decision. Do you quit, or do you double down and put more work in? In those moments remind yourself, this is what growth feels like.

I want to give you a basic Fail Forward Framework that will help you turn your mistakes and "failures" into beneficial experiences. This framework consists of four simple questions to ask yourself whenever you are faced with a challenge or mistake.

1. What Are The Facts Of The Situation?

First, truthfully admit to yourself what happened. Focus on the facts. You will find it is easy to get emotionally invested in the challenges your business faces and you may be tempted to label situations as failures, rejections, or mistakes when in actuality they are just challenges. I want you to clearly tell yourself the facts of what happened.

For example, when I received terrible feedback from my planner design, I felt like the project was a failure. But the fact was that I received negative feedback on a handful of sections on my planner design. I had not failed, I was just faced with a challenge.

2. What Did I Learn?

What lesson did you learn from the experience? Often we are so frustrated by a negative situation that we forget to find the lesson it teaches.

With my focus group, I learned that many of my sections were repetitive. I also learned that focus groups were extremely powerful in helping see problems with my design.

3. How Can I Benefit From This Experience?

Ask yourself, how will this lesson and experience make you better? Once you overcome the challenge in front of you, how will you be better prepared for the future? What new opportunities will be available?

I saw with my planner that, if I made changes based on the feedback, I would have a much better design. I would be able to sell more of them and learn to design winning products.

4. What Actions Will I Take Based On This Lesson?

Looking over the mistake and the lesson, decide how you will change your approach going forward. How will you adjust your plans and actions to avoid more mistakes like this in the future? How can you solve this problem so that you will not have similar ones like it again?

For my planner design, I knew that I needed to make the recommended changes to my planner and keep hosting focus groups until I received consistently good feedback.

Track Your Progress

Whether you are making lots of achievements happen or a bunch of mistakes, you need to be tracking your progress toward your goal. You need a way to reflect on the results of your actions to determine if they are leading you where you want to go, or if you will need to pivot.

For example, let's say you have the goal of making $10,000 worth of sales this month and your plan to make that happen is to make 30 sales calls per day. If after 15 days of working this plan you have only generated $1000 in sales, you would be able to tell you are off track for your goal and that something needs to change. If you weren't tracking your numbers, you wouldn't be able to know whether your plan was working or not and would get frustrated when you didn't reach your target.

Also, tracking your progress and business numbers will bring you new insights. You might realize that 80 percent of your sales came from calling businesses that started less than two years ago. With that insight, you could adjust your plan to target only businesses that are younger than two years old and be much more efficient by calling prospects that are more likely to buy.

As you work on your business, find metrics to track. What are the key measurables you need to be looking at? What actions should you be tracking? What are the results you're hoping to achieve from those actions? Your experts can give you guidance on the best metric to track in your industry. Once you determine the proper metrics to track, it is important to reflect on them regularly so you can learn from their insights.

You will find that it is very easy to get emotionally attached to your business and draw conclusions that may not be true. The beautiful thing is that numbers don't lie. When I started my business I thought it was doing great because I received over $100,000 in revenue in the first six months. But when I looked at the numbers I learned my expenses were over $100,000 and my business was losing money! This was really important to learn so that I could get my spending under control. Numbers don't lie. They can help you make educated decisions rather than emotional ones.

What will be the key metrics for your business to track? How often will you reflect and review them?

Next Steps

After you take time to reflect on your accomplishments, the mistakes, the actions you have taken, and the advice from your experts, look for the next step to take. You will find that when you stop to reflect, the next steps will present themselves. Keep asking yourself, "What is the next indicated step?"

Similar to how you can drive from California to New York in the dark only seeing as far as your headlights, you will also be able to reach your goal by continuously taking the next indicated step. Regular reflection will help reveal a clear path toward your goals.

Reflect And Implement

Reflecting on your actions can make the difference between working efficiently or not, even if it is just for two minutes each day.

- When will you take time to reflect?

_____

_____

_____

Reflect on your accomplishments:

- What have you accomplished so far this year that you are most proud of?
- What new skills have you learned?
- What are some of the biggest challenges you have overcome?
- Who have you helped?
- How have you grown as a person?
- How have you pushed your comfort zone?
- What actions have you taken that you had been procrastinating?

_____

_____

_____

_____

_____

_____

_____

_____

_____

_____

Reflect on your learning experiences

- What mistakes have you made?
- What have you learned from those mistakes?
- How have those lessons benefited you? How have they prepared you?
- How will you act differently based on those lessons?

_____

_____

_____

_____

_____

What are the key metrics that you should use to track your business progress? How often will you review these metrics?

_____

_____

_____

_____

_____

Reflect on your next step:

- Now that you have sought expert counsel and taken action, what is the next indicated step to take?

_____

_____

_____

_____

_____

You can download a free PDF of this exercise at **GoalCrazy.com/ freedownloads**.

Also, if you need help forming the habit of reflection the Goal Crazy Planner has built in questions to help you. You can access a free downloadable sample of this planner at **GoalCrazy.com/freedownloads** or by scanning the QR code below:

PART 3

FIVE STEPS TO LAUNCH YOUR BUSINESS

CHAPTER 16

YOUR ONE-PAGE LAUNCH PLAN

Congrats on making it to this point in the process! You have gone through the Goal Crazy Cycle once and you should now have a winning product or service designed. Be proud of yourself for making it here!

This is where the real fun starts!

You are going to go through all the steps in the Goal Crazy Cycle again, but, this time, with a focus on your business launch.

- You will seek expert counsel to learn the best strategy to launch your business.
- Form a 90 day goal.
- Take messy action.
- Reflect on the actions you take.
- Start the cycle over again until it's launched!

Ideally, you are able to launch your business over the next 90 days, but if it takes longer than that, focus your Most Impactful Goal on a milestone toward launching it.

Launching your business may be one of the most exciting and overwhelming times in your business journey because there is so much to focus on. There is a lot that needs to happen to turn your winning business idea into a profit generating business.

As a whole, getting a business started takes a lot of effort. It will take extra effort in the beginning to gain traction and get the processes moving. So, you want to learn the specific strategies that will help you best get your business "over the hump" and get consistent sales.

Depending on the business, the "launch" may be more or less important. Some businesses require big launch strategies to help the business take off. Others can have a much slower, grow-as-you-go approach.

For example, I have worked with entrepreneurs when launching a product who have a big strategy behind it. They make detailed plans to get press for their businesses, influencers posting about it, giveaways, and podcast appearances. Often the launch can make a big difference in the long-term sales of the product.

I have also worked with other business owners whose launch doesn't need to be as hyped up. For example, the individual who started a web design business that simply drove to a street of businesses and pitched his service to the owners to get sales.

This is why meeting with experts will be so helpful, because they can best guide you to the winning strategies for your industry. However, to give you a framework for your launch I will break the process down into five manageable components that all businesses will need regardless of how big or small your launch strategy is:

- Marketing
- Sales
- Operations
- Funding
- Launch Date

Some components will be more, or less, important for your business, but I will cover all of them. I will put them in the order that I would focus on first, but it's important when you meet with your experts to learn what they believe is most crucial. Obviously they know much more about your specific industry than I do. For each section I will provide example questions you can ask your own expert council to help you compile the information needed for your own successful business launch.

Even though I will provide you with a strategy for launching your business, this does not substitute meeting with experts for advice. Even a perfect book written specifically for your business situation will not replace the value of a good mentor that you can call on. Use this as an opportunity to develop a deeper relationship with the experts you know.

At the end of the chapter, you will find our One-Page Launch Plan that breaks down the five components for your business launch. Fill in each of the five sections as we cover it in the coming chapters. This document will be your guide to organize your launch and help you clarify the key questions to ask your experts to gain the best insights.

Reflect And Implement

Download a free printable copy of our One-Page Launch Plan plus a comprehensive list of sample questions to ask your experts at **GoalCrazy. com/freedownloads** or by scanning the QR code below:

One-Page Launch Plan (front)

Marketing

Free marketing Activities	Expected sales	Method to track sales	Cost
			FREE
			FREE
			FREE
			FREE
			FREE

Paid marketing activites	Expected sales	Method to track sales	Cost

Total expected free and paid sales: _____   **Total marketing costs:** _____

Sales

Questions to uncover **Problems**
_____
_____

Your **Certainty Bridge**
_____
_____

Questions to uncover **Dreams**
_____
_____

Statement or question to close with
_____
_____

Supply

Supplies/inventory needed to launch	Cost	Supplies/inventory continued	Cost

Total supplies/inventory cost: _____

Fullfillment

How will you fulfill sales? _____
Where will you run your business? _____
How will you accept payment? _____
What forms, contracts, or software do you need? _____

Retention

How will you record customer information? _____
How will you follow up with customers? _____
How will you get reviews? _____
How will you handle customer support? _____

GoalCrazy.com

One-Page Launch Plan (back)

Legal Setup

What will your legal structure be? ☐Sole Proprietor ☐Partnership ☐LLC ☐S-corp ☐Other_____

What licenses, permits, trademarks, or forms do you need to legally operate your business?_____
_____

What will you need in order to hire your first employee?_____
_____

How much will it cost to get set up legally?_____

Accounting

How will you handle your bookkeeping and accounting?_____

Do you need to collect and remit sales tax? If so, how will you handle it?_____

What legal steps do you need to take to prepare to hire employees?_____
_____

What other rules, licenses, or regulations are important for your business?_____
_____

Employees

How many employees will you need to launch?_____

How much will it cost?_____

What tools or software will you use to handle employee information and processes?_____
_____

Funding

Calculate Your Startup Costs

1. Inventory/supplies $_____
2. Marketing $_____
3. Operations/software/rent/fulfillment
   $_____
4. Employees $_____
5. Legal $_____
6. Other $_____

Total Startup Cost $_____

Calculate Your Survival Figure
This section is only necessary if you are leaving your job

- How much income do you need each month to cover your core living necessities? $_____

- How many months do you expect it to take for your business to support your needs? _____

- Multiply your core monthly expenses by the number of months to calculate your Survival Figure below.

Survival Figure $_____

Calculate Your Covered Capital Requirement

($ _____ + $ _____) X 2 = $_____

    Total Startup Costs   *Survival Figure*   *Covered Capital Requirement*

Access Capital

How much of your Covered Capital Requirement can you self fund? $_____

How much will you need to raise? $_____

How will you raise the funds? ☐Pre-sells ☐Credit cards ☐Loans ☐Partners ☐Investors ☐Other
_____

Launch

When will you launch your business?_____

What will you do to celebrate your business launch?_____

GoalCrazy.com

CHAPTER 17

CREATE YOUR MARKETING PLAN

As a business owner, one of your primary responsibilities for your early business will be driving sales. If revenue stops, your business will die, so sales needs to be a priority!

It sounds very obvious, but too many entrepreneurs get distracted with all the other demands of their business and stop putting energy into sales. This puts an intense amount of pressure and stress on the business owners when money gets tight.

Even if you have a good product, the proper legal setup, and all the start-up capital you could ever need, if no one buys your products, your business will fail. The sole purpose of the business launch is to drive paying customers to gain traction in the marketplace.

The thing about a new business is that no one knows about it yet. If no one knows you exist, it's impossible for them to buy from you. This is why you *must* focus on drawing attention to business when you launch. Once people are aware of your business, then you can sell them. Having a great marketing plan will spread awareness and spike a boost of sales to get you traction for your business.

When starting your business you will typically find many paid options to market it, as well as free "bootstrap" approaches. Depending on your financial situation, you will choose between the two.

For both free and paid methods, you will see there are unlimited options for marketing, so I'll walk you through just a few basic strategies for each.

I'll teach you my three step process that helps you start with free options, grow into paid options, and track all results to find what works best.

Step One: Start Free

There are a surprising amount of free options to utilize when you're first getting your business started. These options usually require extra time compared to paid options, but when you are first starting, you likely have more time since your business isn't overrun with customers yet. Additionally, since these opportunities are free, they are likely much more profitable sales since you are not spending money on the marketing to acquire them.

I would plan to exhaust all free options to get your business off the ground, then as you start getting regular profits you can dedicate a portion toward paid options to scale. Below are some of my favorite free marketing options.

Friends And Family

One of the easiest marketing avenues is tapping into your current base of friends and family. When you are launching your business you want *everyone* you know to be aware of it. Most likely your friends and family will want to support you and your new business. Just think if a friend of yours decided to open a restaurant, you would *want* to eat there and tell others about it. Your friends and family will be the same way.

Look in your phone right now and see how many contacts you have saved. Look at your social media accounts and see how many followers you have. All of those can be prospects for your business! Even if they are not your target market, they can refer your business to others who are.

When I started my planner business I went through my contacts on my phone, and if I could remember the person's face, I would send a text asking them to purchase my planner and leave a review. I sent a text saying:

Hey _____, I hope you are doing great! I wanted to let you know I launched a business selling planners I designed to help high achievers accomplish their goals. My goal is to get to 100 reviews of my planner during the first two weeks of its launch. If you would be willing to order the planner and leave me a review it would mean the world! It might seem like a small thing, but each review makes a big difference. I will put a link below so you can check it out and share it with others who may enjoy it. Thanks so much!

Not only did this drive initial sales and reviews, but it also opened up a bunch of connections. Some of the people I texted connected me with other online businesses I could collaborate with. Dozens of people posted about my business on their social media to help me gain exposure. One person even helped me get featured on a podcast! They were excited to try and help my business succeed.

You can use this strategy for service based businesses too. Below I will put an example of a text you could send out if you were starting a roofing business.

Hey _____, I hope you are doing well! I wanted to let you know I have started a roofing business. If you need a new roof, or a roof repair, please let me know. Also, if you know anyone who can benefit from my services, be sure to pass my information along. I am happy to provide a free estimate for their roof and during these first couple months I will be offering my most competitive rates. Thank you so much for your consideration!

Even though you will be reaching out to people you personally know with this strategy, it will still push your comfort. Personally, I found this strategy to be extremely frightening when I was starting my business. It seemed vulnerable to reach out to people I knew and asked them for help. It seemed salesy to be asking my friends and family to buy from me. Strangely, I felt more comfortable asking complete strangers to buy my products than my friends. However, after getting such incredible support from those texts, I realized it would have been unfair of me *not* to ask for their help. My friends and family truly wanted to support me.

To implement this strategy I want you to make a list of 100 people you know that you will reach out to during your business launch. If you really want to push this approach, make a list of 1000!

Once you make your list, write a template for a text you can copy and paste and send to them. Then, determine a specified number of texts you will commit to sending each day during your launch week. For example, I sent out ten requests per day for the first two weeks of my launch.

Unfortunately, this strategy is not infinitely scalable. You can reach out to friends and family like this at the start of your business to get support, but after your launch you will need to find other approaches to bring continued growth and sales. That is where the next strategies come in.

Influencers

Wouldn't it be great if you already had a giant following of people in your target market to launch your business to? Luckily, there are influencers that have done this work for you. These could be podcasters, YouTubers, bloggers, or social media accounts that have already built an audience in your niche. Search to find these influencers then offer them a free sample of your product or service to hear their feedback. If they like your product or service, they will likely share it with their audience and you can tap into their customer base for free.

I like to find influencers who have already reviewed similar products to my own, because that indicates they like reviewing products in my niche. Then I track down a way to contact them, whether an email address, phone number, or social media message. I reach out and offer to provide a sample of my product or service to get their feedback.

I did this with my planner business and found dozens of influencers who invited me to speak on their channels as a guest, hosted me on their podcasts, and ultimately put my message in front of thousands of my target customers for free. Here is an example of a message I sent to an influencer.

> *Hey _____,*
>
> *My name is Jason VanDevere, I saw your Youtube channel and thought it was inspiring. I give you a lot of credit for being so open and sharing behind the scenes details about your business. It really makes it easy to understand how to implement your concepts.*
>
> *I also noticed you are a planner lover! I recently designed a planner of my own called Goal Crazy that is based on interviewing dozens of highly successful entrepreneurs.*
>
> *Seeing how passionate you are about planning, goal setting, and productivity, I would love to send you a free copy to see what you think of the design! Let me know where to send it and I will put a planner in the mail for you this week.*
>
> *Thank you so much, keep up the awesome work!*
>
> *Jason VanDevere*
>
> *PS: If you want to learn about the planner first, check it out at: www.goalcrazy.com*

Another approach is to find influencers that have featured the founders of competing brands on their Youtube channels, podcasts, blogs, or social media accounts. If they have enjoyed featuring your competitors, they may likely be interested in featuring you! For example, as I work to promote this book, I will search for podcasts that have featured other authors in my niche on their show and then reach out to see if they would like to feature me as well.

This can also work for local brick and mortar businesses. For example, maybe you want to start a marketing agency for businesses in your town. Ask yourself, who has already gathered the local business owners together? Maybe it is a local BNI (Business Network International) group,

Chamber of Commerce, or Meetup group. Contact the leader to find a way to talk with their members. You could offer to do a free presentation to teach the members simple tricks to improve their marketing. Then use your presentation to connect with the members.

To implement this strategy, create a list of 20 to 100 influencers in your niche. Most influencers will have a website where their contact information can be found. Create an email template that you can send to these influencers to ask for their help. You will likely need to follow up with an influencer several times before you get a reply, so I would keep your list saved in an excel sheet to help organize your notes. You can download a free excel sheet template for this at GoalCrazy.com/freedownloads

Collaborations And Partnerships

This approach works by finding businesses that complement yours, with whom you can create win-win collaboration opportunities. Think of what businesses are already servicing your customers in a different way. For example if you have a business painting houses, it would be helpful to be in contact with a power washing business. They likely meet people regularly who want their house painted, and you likely meet people regularly who prefer to wash their house rather than paint it. You can refer customers to each other.

I have found many other entrepreneurs online who service a similar niche, and we've hosted workshops together that have helped us both. Think to yourself of other complimentary businesses that you could collaborate with. Here is an example for reaching out to them.

> Hey _____, I saw your business and love what you are doing! I have a business that _____ and I thought I might be able to help you out. I have customers who regularly need products/services like yours and I am looking for a good connection to refer them to. Would you be free for a quick phone call sometime this week so I can better understand your

business and find a way to collaborate? I was thinking maybe we could (list example ways you could work together, ex: host a workshop, pay each other commissions for referrals, swap email lists, etc.)

Let me know what you think,

Jason V.

Content Creation

This method will take more time, but you can work to build a following of your own. Start creating valuable content for your target market and post it for free to grow an audience of fans. You could post it on Instagram, Facebook, TikTok, YouTube, blogs, email newsletters, or anywhere that fits with your skill set. This method will take work, but will create a following of fans excited to buy your product or service.

The nice thing is that the work is evergreen. For example, if you build a giant following or email list, you will have it to market to again and again. Unlike paid ads where you can spend thousands of dollars each week, but when you stop spending the money on ads, the sales stop coming in. When you build an organic following, you will have them forever. For example, many ecommerce store owners build large email lists so that they can market products to the list many times in the future.

Networking Events

Networking is extremely helpful if you can find the right network of people. If you are a local business you can likely find a nearby BNI (Business Network International) Group or Chamber of Commerce. There might be other groups more targeted toward your niche too. At these groups you can connect with potential customers, and connect with other business owners who can help refer your business to people they know. You will find if you go with a helpful attitude, they will work hard to support you too.

If you go to these make sure you track how helpful they are. A group that is not the right fit will require your time but not provide any results. But when you find the right group, it will be a win-win for you and the other members.

You can also network online. You can join Facebook groups, forums, and Reddit threads relevant to your niche. You can post regularly and provide value so people start to recognize your name. When you launch your product, you can share it with the group. Just make sure that it's not against the terms for the group you participate in. For example, I had a friend who started a business selling cold plunges. Before he launched his business he was an active member in an ice plunge Facebook group and provided extremely helpful tips and strategies. When he launched his business, he shared it with the group members, and since he was already a respected expert in the group, people were excited to support him.

Press

If you can get your business featured in local newspapers, magazines, TV, radio, or recognized websites, it can create free publicity! Plus, it can provide tremendous social proof for your business. Think of how often you see businesses displaying "As seen on…" and list any trustworthy media outlets where they've been featured.

Getting press will take work, but when you get it, it's free marketing. The smaller the network the easier it will likely be to get featured. Start with the local news and work your way up to larger publications. You can write to them or even stop by their office and tell them about your business. There will be a lot of rejection but getting published once can bring hundreds or even thousands of sales.

Here is an example of an email template to send to an editor at your local news agency:

Hey_____,

My name is Jason VanDevere and I really appreciate your work! I read the recent story you wrote about _____ and loved how you_____. I was reaching out because I have a story that I think your readers would really enjoy.

I just launched a business that _____. I thought it would resonate with your readers because of its unique _____.

Here are a few topic ideas if you wanted to turn it into a story for a future piece.
- *XXXX*
- *XXXX*

Do you think any of these would be a good fit? If so, let me know what information I can provide to help. My schedule is flexible, so I am happy to put in extra work to make this easier for you.

Feel free to email me back or call me at _____.

Talk soon,

Jason VanDevere

Search Engine Optimization

Search engine optimization (SEO) will help your business show up in results when someone searches relevant terms in their search engine (such as Google, Bing, etc.) The better your SEO, the higher your business will rank in the results.

Search engine optimization is free, so when you are making your website make sure you are using a platform that helps optimize it. You can also list your business for free on search engines like Google Business or Yelp so that if someone searches in your area for a business like yours, they will find it.

If you really want to scale this approach, you can invest money into this by paying for tools or agencies that specialize in getting your business to rank better.

Affiliate

Affiliates are influencers who market your products in exchange for a commission of the sales they send your way. Technically they are paid since they get a portion of the revenue, but you only pay them if they bring you sales. There is no cost upfront, which is why I am putting this in the free section. It's extremely easy to implement if you have an ecommerce website. Most of the leading ecommerce web design platforms have built in features to facilitate this. Basically your affiliates will create an account on your website which will generate either a unique link or promo code that they can share with their audience. The site will then track the sales they send your way and pay them a commission. When you find the right influencer this becomes a beautiful win-win-win relationship. They are able to earn money off their giant following, you are able to gain new customers, and the customers receive your amazing products or services.

You could use this approach for brick and mortar businesses too, you will just need to find a way to track where your leads came from. Such as giving your affiliate coupons to pass out so that you could pay the affiliate commissions when someone uses their coupon.

Cold Calling

This last approach is a grind, but it works if you are willing to do it. You can simply cold call your prospective customers. Whether you call them on the phone, email them, or knock on their door, this approach will have you reaching out to your ideal customers and asking for the sale. For example if you want to start a web design business you can simply visit or call local businesses and offer your services. You will experience rejection along the way, but it is free, aside from your time.

Step Two: Test Paid

After you've exhausted your free marketing options you can look at the paid ones. Often new business owners tell me, "I don't want to spend thousands of dollars on ads."

Typically when I hear this, I ask a simple question, "Let's say I had a magic box that doubled your money. If you put $1 in, then $2 would come out. If you put $1000 in, $2000 would come out. If I let you borrow this box for a month, how much money would you put into it?" Typically they respond with, "I would put as much money as I could into it."

Here's the thing, when you find a winning ad campaign it will do the same thing. You can spend $100 on ads and generate $200 in profit. You can spend $10,000 on ads and generate $20,000 in profit. I don't want you to lose thousands of dollars on marketing either, but when you find the right campaigns you will have the opportunity to double, triple, or quadruple each dollar you spend. Maybe even more! And when you have that, you will *want* to spend thousands of dollars each month.

The reason this section is called "test" paid ads is because you will have to do exactly that. You will have to test many ads to find the ones that work. You may launch ten campaigns and find nine lose money and only one turns a profit. You will need to kill the losing campaigns and multiply the winning ones. It often takes many attempts to find a winning campaign. I view this process as an investment. Even though many of your early campaigns may lose money, this is the investment you put in to create the winning campaigns you desire. View all of your campaigns as buying information to see which campaigns will work well and which will not. Having a good expert contact can help you greatly flatten the learning curve, but either way you will need to experiment to find the winners.

If you launch paid ads and they don't work at first, I do not want you to think they'll never work. The point of this section is not to test whether paid ads will work for your business. They *can* work, you just need to experiment until you find the right campaigns for you. Here are several different popular paid advertising options.

Social Media Ads

Social media sites are an incredible way to market to new customers. Platforms like Facebook, Instagram, LinkedIn, TikTok, and YouTube are extremely powerful. You can target niche groups of people and track whether those people click your ad, view the page, and purchase. It gives you detailed metrics to help you see which ads are working and which are not.

You'll need to decide for yourself if marketing on these platforms will be a skill that you want to learn for yourself or hire out. You can find freelancers to run your ads on sites like Upwork or Fiverr for relatively cheap.

Search Engine Ads

Another phenomenal tool is Google Ads. I'll put YouTube in here again because it functions largely like a search engine. On these platforms you can target specific search terms for your business. Think of what your target market might be searching for on Google or YouTube. You can tailor your ads so your business will show up for those people's search results.

Paid Influencer Marketing

Although you can find smaller influencers for free, if you want to go after the large ones, you will likely have to pay them to market your business. In my experience, influencers targeted to my niche are worth the investment.

I prefer to invest in influencer content that is "evergreen." By evergreen, I mean that it will be around forever. For example, a YouTube video or blog post will get a large amount of views when it is published but it will also remain out there forever. YouTube videos or blog posts people made for me six years ago still get views today because people still find them in search results. However, if I compare this to "non-ever green" content, such as a social media post or being featured on someone's Instagram story, those will not be relevant forever. If someone posts about my business in their feed today, in a week that post is buried by new posts and will likely disappear.

Not that these aren't also helpful, because they can certainly work to bring a spike in sales. But the evergreen opportunities spike sales *and* maintain a trickle of sales continuing into the future.

Step Three: Track Results

The key to all of these ads is to track your results. Too often businesses engage in many different marketing activities but have no way of tracking where their sales are coming from. This makes it impossible for them to know which activities to scale and which to kill.

For each marketing approach you want to implement, work to predict the expected amount of sales you believe you can generate from that approach. Your experts will be extremely helpful for this because they have personal experience with the approaches you are interested in. Once you create a sales target for the approach, find a way to track the method's results so you can see if it performs as expected.

I always want to have my ads trackable in some way. For example, I give different promo codes to different ads or influencers I am using so I can track which promo codes are used the most. I have different links attached to different ads so I can see which links are generating the most clicks.

Even for local businesses, you can create different phone numbers to track which is driving customers. You can create "virtual numbers" that redirect to your phone. Google Voice allows you to make one for free, but other paid virtual number apps, such as CallRail, allow you to make many more.

Let's pretend you have a gutter cleaning business and you want to track where your leads are coming from. You can create three different phone numbers; the first you can put on your Google ads, the second you can put on yard signs, and a third you can put on your social media pages. All three numbers will redirect the calls to your cell phone, but when people call you, you will know how they heard of your business. You can determine which ads are bringing in the leads.

You can also make it part of your process to ask your new prospects how they heard about your business. This is not always entirely accurate because people may forget, but if you do get consistent answers, you can better determine your winning strategies.

Either way, you want to predict the expected sales you will get from various marketing activities, and find a way to track which marketing activities generate the most profitable sales.

Find Your Experts

During your launch phase, work hard to find good experts and learn about how they marketed their products during their launch. It is helpful to learn from those who have bootstrapped their way to success, and others who had deeper pockets to buy their place in the market. Both are good to learn from.

As you start to learn their strategies, try to determine how many sales you can expect to generate from the marketing efforts. This will give you direction for how you need to build the proper processes to handle the launch and fulfill all the sales as they come in.

Here are some questions to guide your conversation with your expert council:

- How do you market your business?
- How did you gain your first clients?
- Did you do anything special for your business launch to gain exposure? What worked well and what didn't? What would you do differently if you were doing it again?
- What were some free ways you gained exposure for your business?
- What were some paid marketing strategies that worked well?
- Did you run the marketing campaigns yourself or hire someone to do it?
- How many sales should I expect at the start of my business?

- How long did it take for sales to start consistently coming in?

- Did you run any discounts for your launch that helped drive sales?

Reflect And Implement

Fill out the Marketing portion of the One-Page Launch Plan based on the exercises in this chapter. Make note of key questions you have so you can discuss the topics with your experts for guidance.

If you have not accessed your One-Page Launch Plan yet, download it free at **GoalCrazy.com/freedownloads** or by scanning the QR code below:

CHAPTER 18

YOUR SALES PROCESS

Once your marketing efforts start gaining attention, you need a plan to convert that interest into sales and generate revenue. For many, the idea of selling can leave a bad taste in your mouth—even the word "sales" itself might feel uncomfortable or off-putting.

If this is you, I want to provide you with a new approach that will allow you to sell your product or service without being salesy. For you to be able to understand how this approach works, you will need to first understand the power of quality questions.

I didn't fully understand the power of quality questions until I started selling planners. People have used my planner to accomplish a wide range of goals, such as starting businesses, losing weight, graduating from college, or even homeschooling their kids. The crazy thing about it though, is that my planner provides the users with *no* answers. It does not give any solutions to their problems. Rather, it only has *questions*. The planner utilizes powerful questions to help the user understand what they want to accomplish and how to accomplish it. It asks questions like:

- What would you love to achieve?
- Why do you want that?
- What could you do for 15 minutes every day to move you closer to that goal?

Quality questions like this help the users organize their thoughts so they can be better understood. This clarity untaps motivation within them to act on their desires.

I mention this because a true sales professional does exactly that. Instead of letting a customer's thoughts and desires remain jumbled and unclear, you can ask the right questions to help them organize and articulate what they're feeling. Once they gain that clarity, making the decision to buy becomes much easier.

For a sales professional, understanding is the key! I do *not* mean helping the customer only understand the benefits of what you sell—that is an old-school approach. Rather, I mean helping them understand their own needs. When you can help the customer fully understand their own needs, it leads to three wonderful outcomes:

1. When a customer understands how to solve their problems they naturally gain motivation to fix them. The customer will *want* to buy a solution without the need to be "sold."
2. When you help a customer understand their needs, they feel understood and will be more likely to follow your guidance.
3. If you realize you do not have the appropriate solution for the customer's needs, it will be obvious to both you and the customer. Rather than attempting hard pressure closing tactics on a customer that is not the right fit, you will be able to confidently point them in the direction of a more appropriate solution. This will build trust and the customers will be more likely to come back to you again if they ever need your help in the future.

Depending on the type of business you have, the exact strategy to implement this sales process will vary. There is a different process I use to sell planners online, coaching programs over the phone, or vacant apartments in person. Since there is so much variation, I want to cover a few key concepts of the sales process that apply in a wide variety of situations. I want to cover the Problem, Dream, Bridge method of selling. This approach can work for selling in-person, over the phone, or through written copy, such as on a website or email.

Remember, the best selling practices for your business will come from your experts. You can learn from them how to best implement this for your situation.

Problem

As we discussed when you were designing your product or service, people buy things that solve problems. If a customer doesn't acknowledge they have a problem, they will be extremely unlikely to buy a solution. So, the first step in the process is to help the customer clearly identify the problem they need help solving. Even though you might already know the problem the customer has, you need to ask quality questions that allow the customer to acknowledge it for themselves.

Asking questions like this provides a tremendous amount of benefit to the customer because it will allow them to reflect on their life and business to analyze the source of their problems. It also benefits you because the answers will help you better understand the customer's needs.

Here are some example questions you can ask:

- What challenges are you currently facing?
- What about your current solution frustrates you?
- Are you currently experiencing (insert common problem your customers have)?

You can use questions like this when selling in-person, over the phone, or even in written copy too. The sales page for my planner starts with questions such as "Are you working hard but not making progress?" and "Stuck with endless to-do lists with no time to complete them?" Even though I cannot hear the prospect's responses, the questions still allow them to acknowledge their problems to themselves.

Once your prospect shares with you the current challenges they are facing, it's now time to use expanding questions to encourage the prospect to elaborate more on the implications of the details they shared. Expanding questions make the prospect feel the pain of the problems they have. They reveal the costs of their problems so that the need for your solution is more obvious. For example, you can ask questions like:

- What is the worst part about that?
- How much money/time/effort/stress is this problem costing you?
- How long has that been going on?
- What happens if nothing is done to change this?
- How does this affect the other areas of your life/business?
- How does this make you feel?

The answers to these questions will help you fully understand their problem. Often the first problem they share with you, is not the true problem. The problem they shared likely has implications or costs that are causing the most pain to the customer. Expanding questions will help reveal them.

For example, when I was selling cars, I once had a retired couple come in and share with me that they needed a new vehicle because their current one was having issues. After I asked a few expanding questions, they shared how their current vehicle had broken down on the side of the road twice over the past year causing over $2000 in repairs. Because of this, they were afraid to drive the vehicle more than ten miles from home, preventing them from seeing their grandkids.

As you can see, the expanding questions helped me realize that under their initial problem of "having vehicle issues," was a much larger problem of not being a good grandparent. I helped them realize that many of the challenges they were facing were coming from their vehicle. They could see that they wouldn't just be buying a vehicle, they would be freeing themselves from the ten-mile prison they were trapped in!

When you ask your initial problem identifying questions, you learn *what* the customers' issues are. But, when you ask the expanding questions, you learn *why* it is a problem. This will be the motivation that leads them to buy, so you need to ask quality questions that will clarify it.

Dream

Next, we need to clarify the dream the prospect has. We need to understand what their ideal solution would be. This will help you and the customer determine if your solution can create this dream of theirs. I will put example questions below you can use to do this:

- What is the outcome you are trying to create?
- If this issue were fixed, what would your life or business be like?
- What would your ideal solution be?

Once you clarify the dream they have, you can use expanding questions again to clarify their dream further. This time, you will use these questions to help the prospect clarify the benefit of their dream rather than the pain of their problems. This will help you fully understand the vision they want, and it will help motivate the customer to take the actions to make it happen.

You can ask questions like:

- What would be the best part about having this?
- How much money/time/effort/stress will this save you?
- How will this impact other areas of your life/business?
- What new opportunities would be on your horizon when you have something like this in place?
- What would be the biggest benefit of having a solution like this?
- How would it feel to have this?

When I was selling cars, people would often share with me they desired a bigger vehicle. I would then ask expanding questions like, "What would be the best part about that? What would you use the extra space for? What types of trips would you now be able to take?"

The customer would share an entirely new lifestyle of travel, carpooling, and freedom they could have. Rather than me simply selling them a vehicle, I was opening them up to a new way of life! From there, they had their own internal motivation to buy the vehicle. Any sales tactics became unnecessary because the customer *wanted* to make the purchase.

Expanding questions can have the same impact for you! Think of questions that will allow your customers to clarify the *why* behind their dream. This is what motivates them to buy! And it will provide you with better clarity for you of the exact type of solution the customer wants.

Bridge

It is now time to position your product or service as the bridge that will take the prospect from the challenging situation they are in to the dream they want.

Obviously, if you do not have the right product or service to fix their solution, then be honest and point them in another direction. If you *can* solve their problem though, then express that! Show them how you can help create their dream.

There will be three parts to bridging your customer from the problem they are in to the dream they want:

1. Certainty Statement
2. Solution Process
3. The Close

1. Certainty Statement

Customers want *certainty* that your solution will solve their problem. The more certain they are, the more likely they are to buy. So, create a Certainty Statement that expresses your total conviction in the solution you have to offer.

A Certainty Statement is a short sentence that expresses complete conviction that you can bridge the gap from the customer's problem to their dream. For example:

- I am 100% confident I can help you with this…
- This is precisely the type of challenges our product will solve…
- Our solution makes this exact transformation possible…

You can amplify the power of your Certainty Statement by using reviews of past clients. If you are selling online, you can include testimonials on your sales page to show the validity to your claims. If you are selling in-person or on the phone, you can mention a past customer that had similar challenges and share how they overcame the challenges using your product or service.

Another way you can prove the validity of your Certainty Statement is to offer a guarantee or warranty. These confirm the truth of your claim because if you fail to live up to it, the customer has a guarantee to rely on.

After you deliver your Certainty Statement, explain your Solution Process.

2. Solution Process

Your Solution Process will break down the steps of *how* your product or service will get them from where they are to where they want to be.

If the solution you are selling is complex, try your best to simplify your Solution Process into two to five steps. If you are selling web design services, rather than explaining to the prospect 15 steps in your process, make a general three step outline. For example, "First I will do an audit of your current website and your industry. Second, I will make a draft of the new website for you to experiment with and try for several days. Third, I make reversions to the design until it perfectly fits your needs and the needs of your customers." People love simple, so demonstrate the ease of your offering.

Focus on highlighting the benefits of your product or service, not just the features. The features are the facts of *what* your product or service has to offer. The benefits are *why* the customer cares. A feature of the Goal Crazy planner is that it has a habit tracker. The benefit is that it holds the user accountable to take action and therefore get results. Benefits are ultimately what the customer is purchasing.

3. The Close

Once you help the customer understand your Solution Process, you can close the sale by asking them to purchase. Once they agree to purchase, the deal is "closed."

You will find that if you follow this process, closing the sale should be a breeze because the customer will see how buying your product or service *is* solving their problem. By deciding to buy, they are bridging themselves from the problems they have to the dreams they want. Customers will be hungry to purchase and ask to move forward. However, if you try to close before you've fully clarified the customer's problem and dream, closing will be a struggle and the customer will need convincing in order to do business with you.

When closing the sale, I avoid using yes-or-no questions such as, "Do you want to buy?" I prefer to assume the sale and close with an either-or-question, or simply direct them to take the next step to finalize the sale. For example:

- Would you prefer option A, B, or C?
- Go ahead and sign here and here so I can get the process rolling for you.

Remember, the most important person to sell is yourself. If you truly believe in your product or service your conviction will sell it better than any of your words. When you see the value in your product or service, you will naturally do all you can to make the sale because you will understand the positive impact it can make on your customer's lives.

Questions to Ask Your Experts

The best sales strategies for your industry will come from your experts. There might be a completely different approach to selling in your industry, so speaking with experts will be key. Below are example questions you can ask your experts:

- How do you turn your leads into sales?
- What is your sales process or pitch like?
- How do you present your product or service so customers see the value?
- How do you help customers realize they need a product or service like yours?
- How do you guide the customer to decide to buy today?

Reflect And Implement

Fill out the Sales portion of the One-Page Launch Plan based on the exercises in this chapter. Make note of key questions you have so you can discuss the topics with your experts for guidance.

Additionally you can download a template for a sales script and a sales webpage that uses this framework at **GoalCrazy.com/freedownloads** or by scanning the QR code below:

SCAN ME

CHAPTER 19

BUSINESS OPERATIONS AND LEGAL SETUP

As sales start coming in, you'll need a clear plan for the logistics of how you will actually deliver on what you sell. What will the process look like to deliver a quality experience for your customer in a timely manner, all while keeping yourself organized?

With my planner business, I needed to design what the process would look like to warehouse the planners and have them mailed to the customers after they placed an order. I wanted a process so that the customer would get automatic emails with their tracking information along with access to a training area with videos to help them. Plus, I wanted a way to keep all information from my customers and orders organized.

In this section, I will help you clarify how you will handle the basic operations for your business. Depending on your business type there will likely be software, forms, and processes to utilize. This can take time to set up initially, but will make everything easier as your business grows.

You don't need to have a world class process right away, but you do want to have some basics in place so you can quickly deliver on sales as they come in. Creating written processes to deliver on your products and services will make your business much easier to grow. Without them, you will quickly get disorganized and limit your potential.

A few years ago, I worked with a lawn mowing company. The business owner kept track of everything for his business "in his head." Each morning, my client woke up and texted his brother a list of properties to mow that day. Periodically throughout the month, he read through those prior text messages to see the properties they had mowed. Then he would text his clients to let them know how much money they owed him and wait for his customers to mail him payment.

Technically, he did have a process in place—it was just a terrible one. Because he kept track of everything in his head, he often forgot to bill clients or even failed to mow all the properties he had because the business was disorganized. This made him stressed, overwhelmed, and limited his growth because he wasted hours trying to track down customer information.

Luckily there is software out there designed specifically for landscapers that will track clients, billing, and scheduling. Simply establishing the process of using software rather than purely his memory saved him hours each day and made his business scalable.

What process will you establish? When a customer wants to buy, what will you do? How will you accept payment? How will you keep track of your sales? How will you record your expenses? How will you deliver on the product or service? Are there contracts or forms that your customers need to sign? How will you keep track of all your accounting?

These are some basic questions to think about, but the answers can quickly come from your expert counsel. Find experts who are organized and ask them about their processes. With a proper process your business can become scalable and passive. Without any processes you will be overworked, overwhelmed, and stressed trying to keep track of everything. Especially if you have employees, they will scale the chaos even quicker.

Below are six key areas of your business operations to think about as well as potential questions you can ask your experts to learn the best strategies for each. You do not need to ask all of these questions, just focus on the areas where you need the most help.

1. Supply

You'll want a basic plan of where to get your inventory or your job supplies. Figure out how long it takes to receive them so you can plan accordingly and have enough to cover your launch sales.

Questions to ask your experts council:

- How did you find a supplier for your inventory/job supplies?
- How long does it take to get your inventory/job supplies?
- How much supply should I get to prepare for my launch?
- What supplies will I need?

2. Fulfillment

You'll want a basic process to fulfill sales as they come in. Decide how you will accept payment. If you want to accept credit cards, there are easy tools like Stripe or Square to help. If you'll need contracts or forms, eForms.com is a helpful resource to get free templates. (Obviously consult with a lawyer for any legal documents.) Research software in your industry that can help keep you organized. If you need help making a website, tools like Wix.com, Squarespace, or Shopify are great. You can even hire a freelancer on Upwork.com to make you a site for cheap if you don't want to do the work yourself.

You'll also need to determine where you will run your business out of. Will you run this out of your house, or do you need to rent an office, building, or warehouse? To help find inexpensive opportunities to rent space you can look in your city to find "coworking spaces" or "startup incubators." These are great options for new businesses to gain access to resources without spending much money.

Questions to ask your experts council:

- What type of space will I need to run this business out of? How can I find the best location?
- When someone buys from you how do you fulfill the sale of that product or service?

- How do you accept payment from your customers?
- Are there any contacts, forms, or sales agreements I need in place to launch?
- What software do you recommend to help with the fulfillment of my sales?
- Do you think I need a website for my business when I launch? How did you make yours?

3. Retention

You need a clear way to organize all of your customer information and follow up with your customers for the future. This will allow you to provide customer support, sell to your customers again, get reviews, and more.

Questions to ask your experts:

- After you deliver on the product or service, how do you keep track of your customers for the future?
- How do you follow up to support them and sell to them again?
- Is there software or a CRM that you recommend to organize customers' data?
- How do you get reviews from your customers? Have you found them to be helpful?
- What are the common issues customers need support with after the sale? How do you handle these customer support issues as they arise?

4. Legal Setup

As you are starting your business you will have to decide the legal structure you want to operate under. For example you need to decide if you want to operate as a sole proprietorship, a partnership, LLC, S-corp, C-corp, etc. Unfortunately I cannot provide any legal advice, so you will want to rely on your experts, lawyers, and accountants to guide you.

Depending on the business you're starting, this might be something you want to do right away, or for other businesses maybe it is fine to operate as a sole proprietorship when starting out and can grow into another entity as your business grows.

Let's break this down into three easy steps: Research, Decide, Act.

i. Research

Research the best legal setup for your business type and size. Ask your experts what they would recommend. Also, ask for contacts they know who can help you. You will likely have to pay for these legal services so do your best to learn what is necessary at the start and what can wait until you have business profits coming in. You can use services like LegalZoom to get inexpensive basic legal advice for your business.

If you are hiring employees, I would *highly* recommend consulting a lawyer to make sure you are set up properly first. You want to make sure you have the right contracts, disclosures, policies and documents to protect you and your employees.

Here are some questions to help discuss this with your experts.

- What legal business structure would you recommend when just starting out? Sole proprietorship, partnership, LLC, S-corp, etc.
- Are there any licenses I need before I start? If so, how do I go about obtaining them?
- Who would you recommend me reach out to to help me get legally set up to operate?
- Are there permits I need specific to this industry? If so, how do I file for them?
- Will I need a copyright, trademark, or patent for this type of work? How do I go about attaining those? How long will it take? How much will it cost? Who do you recommend I contact to help me obtain them?
- What will I need in order to hire my first employee?
- What do I need to launch my business versus what can wait until after I have my business running and established?

ii. Decide

Decide what will be necessary to file and complete before you launch your business, versus what can wait until after you have launched your business, further proved the concept, and started receiving revenue. Maybe it is perfectly fine for you to operate the business under your personal name while just starting out. This is why expert counsel is so helpful—they can protect you from wasting time (and money) on unnecessary activities.

iii. Act

Use the advice, contacts, and resources provided from your research to take the required legal steps to get your business ready to launch.

Remember that just because you form an LLC, it does not mean you actually have a business.

Yes, getting the right legal entity is important, but too often I see people get distracted with these details before they have a product or service ready. They get excited about their business idea and form an LLC, set up bank accounts, form operating agreements and contracts to use, but then never actually finish designing their product or service. Be careful of this! The goal is a profitable business, not an empty LLC.

5. Accounting

Keeping the books for your business is important. Not only will it help you make informed decisions, but it will be necessary for when you file your taxes. Software like Quickbooks or Xero makes the process simple by linking directly to your bank account and sales channels to categorize expenses. You can learn this skill yourself or hire it out. I have found cost effective bookkeepers on Upwork to help do this for me.

In addition to bookkeepers, it is also helpful to meet with a CPA or accountant to learn the rules and regulations for your industry. A good accountant can help you save thousands of dollars on your taxes and help you make sure your business is financially set up properly. They can give you guidance for paying employees, collecting and remitting sales tax, setting aside money for your income tax, and much more.

If you are going to hire employees, meeting with a CPA will be extremely helpful to make sure you have your business setup to handle payroll and all of its components like Federal Income Tax, Medicare, unemployment tax, etc. It might seem overwhelming your first time, but once you get a system setup to handle it, it's straightforward from there.

Questions to ask your expert:

- How do you handle your bookkeeping and accounting? Do you have a bookkeeper or CPA you recommend?
- Is there software you recommend for this?
- Do I need to collect and remit sales tax? If so, what are the best tools and strategies to handle it?
- What will I need to file and pay for my employees? Who can help me do this?
- What other rules, licenses, or regulations should I be aware of for my business?
- How much money should I set aside to pay my income tax?

6. Employees

Maybe you will need employees from the start or maybe that will come after your business is more established. Software like Gusto, Quickbooks, and ADP can make it easier to onboard and pay your staff.

Questions to ask your experts council:

- When did you start hiring employees?
- How do you find good applicants?
- How do you manage your team?
- What is their payplan based on?
- How do you handle your payroll? Are there software programs or accountants you recommend?
- How do you communicate effectively with a team?

Reflect And Implement

Fill out the Operation portions (Supply, Fulfillment, Retention, Legal Setup, Accounting and Employees) of the One-Page Launch Plan based on the exercises in this chapter. Make note of key questions you have so you can discuss the topics with your experts for guidance.

If you have not accessed your One-Page Launch Plan yet, download it free at GoalCrazy.com/freedownloads or by scanning the QR code below:

CHAPTER 20

FUND YOUR BUSINESS
AND LAUNCH IT!

The last thing you want to do is start your business and run out of cash to operate it just short of having it gain traction. It's helpful to learn roughly how much you will need to invest into your business before it becomes profitable and how long that might take. You can learn from your experts how much it will cost to start and if there are financing options available.

Ideally, try to find someone who started a similar business to yours and was in a similar financial situation. If you have little to no money to invest, look for someone who began their business with minimal funds. If you have a significant amount of start-up capital, find someone who also had a generous budget when they launched theirs. The strategies between these two scenarios will differ, so finding the one most relevant to your situation will be most helpful.

There are two steps to plan out the funding for your business. First, we need to calculate how much money you will need to launch your business. Secondly, we will need to access the money. I will guide you through both.

Step One: Calculate Your Startup Capital Requirements

Total Startup Costs

The first step will be to calculate how much money you need to cover all your startup costs. I will list out several of the common areas of expense for a new business. For each, identify how much you expect to pay to get your business launched.

- Inventory/Job supplies $_____
- Marketing $_____
- Software/Website/Fulfillment/Rent $_____
- Employees $_____
- Legal $_____
- Other $_____
- Total Startup Costs _____

Survival Figure

If you plan to quit your job to start your business and have no other source of income to cover your basic bills, then also factor in how much money you will need to live off of until your business can support you. I call this your Survival Figure, which represents how much money you need to pay your absolutely necessary bills (rent/mortgage, groceries, utilities, insurance, transportation, etc) while you are starting your business.

To calculate this, total your absolutely necessary monthly living expenses, then multiply it by the number of months you expect it to take to get your business consistently producing profits high enough to support your needs. For example, if you have monthly personal expenses of $2000 per month and you expect it to take three months to get your business producing consistent profits, you will need an additional $6000 to support yourself during that time.

If you plan to keep your full-time job, or have a part-time job to provide for your basic necessities, then this Survival Figure can be $0.

Covered Capital Requirement

Using the pieces of information you gather, we will calculate your total Covered Capital Requirement. This is how much money you will need to cover your startup costs, living expenses, and give you some additional funds to cover unexpected expenses that may arise.

First let's add your Total Startup Costs and Survival Factor together to calculate your *Optimistic* Capital Requirement. That is, if everything goes exactly as planned, that is how much money you will need to fund your business.

Total Startup Costs + Survival Factor = Optimistic Capital Requirement

However, you will likely run into challenges, so I would add some buffer in there. In my experience, it typically takes two to three times more money, time, and work to start a business than initially expected. Make sure you have plans in place to handle this if it happens to you. To do this, take your Optimistic Capital Requirement and multiply it by two. This will represent your Covered Capital Requirement. Your Covered Capital Requirement is the amount of capital you will need to cover your startup costs, survival needs, *and* cover unforeseen challenges that unfold.

Optimistic Capital Requirement x 2 = Covered Capital Requirement

For example, if you had a Total Startup Cost of $4000 and I had a Survival Factor of $6000 then your Optimistic Capital Requirement would be $10,000. But, to help cover any surprise challenges that present themselves, double this number to $20,000. This will provide a buffer to help cover unforeseen challenges, expenses, and setbacks when starting your business, which are very likely to happen!

I know that raises the amount of necessary capital significantly, but I would much rather you have extra cash than to shut down your business because you ran out of cash a few months before your business started to catch on. Obviously it's best to ask the experts in your industry how much extra cash they recommend you have to cover unexpected expenses.

Maybe they think doubling your startup funds is way too much, but maybe they recommend you save up even more!

Calculate Your Covered Capital Requirement now. This will represent the total amount of money you need to get your business started.

Step Two: Access Capital

Now that we calculated how much money you will need, let's make a plan to get it. To fund your business you ultimately have two options: you can fund it with your own money or you can fund it with outside money.

Self Funded

If you can fully self fund your business, that is terrific. That will remove the need to pay back debt to lenders which can remove financial stress for your business. I would recommend you take your startup funds and move them into a new bank account specifically for your business. This will help remove the temptation to spend the money on other unnecessary expenses, plus will help to keep your business and personal money separate.

If you want to self fund your business, but do not have enough cash to do it now, you will want to start saving up money. You can access a free guide to help you make a savings plan at GoalCrazy.com/freedownloads.

Outside Funding

There are many of you who do not want to wait to save up the money to start your business and yet do not have all the necessary startup capital required. For that reason, I want to give strategies to raise the money. First we will need to determine how much money you will need.

Subtract the amount of money you have saved up to invest into your business from the Covered Capital Requirement. For example, if you need $20,000 and you have $5000 saved up, you need to find an additional $15,000 to get your business started.

I will warn you that using outside capital can be riskier, which is why it is so important to have a business you are passionate about. When you have a business you are passionate about you will be much more willing to take on risk to make your business happen. Below I will list out several ways to raise the necessary funds.

1. Presell

The preferred method to raise funds for your business is to presell your products or services. For example, if you want to start a roofing business and need $15,000 to buy the necessary equipment and supplies, you could presell several roofing jobs to raise the funds to buy the equipment. That way you do not need to take on any debt or give away equity in your business to investors.

Additionally, there are platforms that help you do this like Kickstarter.com and Indiegogo.com. These platforms help you "crowdsource" your startup funds by allowing you to list your product or service and letting others preorder it, or simply contribute money toward your mission.

2. Zero APR Credit Cards

I was hesitant to list this as an option because it is *high* risk. However, since I personally used this strategy while starting Goal Crazy, and I have met so many other entrepreneurs that have used it to start their businesses, I felt like I had to mention it. Basically there are credit cards out there that give you an intro rate of 0 percent APR. Often this is for 12 to 18 months, meaning you can get the credit card, buy thousands of dollars of purchases for your business, and have 12 to 18 months to pay it back with *no* interest. If you have reasonable credit, these cards are typically easy to get. I have seen people get approved for $5000 to even $25,000. Sometime more! I have even seen friends take out several of these cards at the same time. For example they might get one with Chase, one with AMEX and one with Capital One. This opens up thousands of dollars of funding.

Again, this is *high* risk, because after your 0 percent APR period ends, you will get moved to an extremely high interest rate. Entrepreneurs I have seen successfully do this buy their startup expenses on the credit card, then work their butt off to pay it back before the 0 percent intro period ends. I used this strategy to fund inventory when I first started Goal Crazy and the fear of encurring a high interest rate on the card gave urgency to sell my products quickly and profitably so that I could pay the card off way before the 0 percent intro rate ended.

3. Loans

Another way to raise money for your business is to get loans. Often financing a new business can be difficult, but there are programs out there such as Small Business Administration (SBA) Loans from the government. Ask your experts for guidance in your industry about the best loan opportunities.

If you are struggling to get approved for a business loan you can look at getting a personal loan. I have also seen people refinance money out of their house or car to start their business. Obviously these are riskier because you have more to lose.

Once you get a business started and profitable, it is much easier to get a loan to grow an existing business than it is to fund a brand new business idea. Use this to your advantage! If you cannot seem to get approved for your loan, try to launch just a portion of your business on a smaller scale. Then after you run that business, apply for a loan to grow the business into your full dream. For example, I met an entrepreneur who wanted to start a restaurant but could not get approved for a large enough loan. So, he decided to open a food truck and started selling at gatherings in his town. After a year or two of running his food truck, he was approved for a loan to expand into a restaurant. Not only did this help him get financing, but he learned incredible lessons from his time in the food truck that helped his restaurant succeed.

Another option is to look at purchasing a business rather than starting one from scratch. Often it is easier to get approved for a loan to buy an existing business because the business will have a proven track record that reduces the lender's risk. I have seen people get approved with less money down and more favorable financing terms. You will have to decide if this approach aligns with your personal goals for your business or not. If it does, you can search on websites like BizBuySell or BizQuest for businesses similar to the one you want to start. Additionally, I would highly recommend the book *Buy Then Build* by Walker Deibel to learn a successful approach to acquiring profitable businesses like this.

4. Partnerships

Another method is to partner with someone who has startup capital. I have met entrepreneurs where one of the partners funds the business while the other partner provides "sweat equity" by working for the business. This may or may not align with your long-term personal goals for your business ownership. However, if you are open to this, think of who you know that has money and might want to start a business. Their role can be much more passive than yours because they will be responsible for the cash and financial advice, while your role is to put in the work.

The nice thing about this opportunity is it can also provide you the opportunity to get coaching from someone more experienced than you. For example, if you have a rich friend who started a large business, and he now wants to become a partner in your business, he will likely also become a mentor to make sure his investment is safe.

5. Friends, Family, And Investors

Maybe you cannot seem to get approved for financing anywhere, or you simply don't want to borrow money from a big institution. That is where friends and family come in. You can ask people you know to invest in your business. You can offer to pay them a specific interest rate or even offer them equity in your business in exchange.

You can also ask people you don't know to invest into your business. You can find angel investors or investment groups that specialize in your industry. Investors typically want a stake in the company in exchange for the money. Angel investors will fall outside the scope of this book, but luckily there are many books out there dedicated to raising money from investors like this. If you are interested in this approach, I recommend you start by finding people who have raised money like this in the past, as they will give you much better guidance than me.

Extra Tips For Raising Startup Funds

Raising startup capital is a big mental and real life hurdle that prevents many aspiring entrepreneurs from starting. To overcome this, getting a good expert council will be key! Use *all* the strategies from Chapter Eight to find experts. Connect with business owners in your space to learn how they financed their business. Call lenders even if you think you are likely to get declined for a loan. Call and ask questions to learn what they look for in a business like yours. Pitch your business to investors, friends, and family to ask for funds. If they tell you, "no," then ask them, "why." Ask them what they would need to see in your business idea to give them the confidence to invest into it. This can reveal strategies to both improve your pitch and help you identify potential threats to your business model that are making it risky.

Additionally, look up companies similar to the one you want to start and research their founder. Search online to see if their founder was ever interviewed on a podcast or YouTube channel telling their startup story. You can likely learn from them the strategies they were able to use to fund their business. There are thousands of entrepreneurs out there who have started massive companies with little to nothing, and their strategies and stories can help you do the same.

Remember, action brings clarity. Once you start having conversations with experts and researching strategies for your industry, the path to success will get clearer. The more funds you are trying to raise, the more action it will likely take to raise them. Additionally the more rejection, deadends, and challenges will likely arise. However, the resilience you build while raising your startup capital will be the same resilience needed to make your business a success once you start it. Your journey to startup capital will be the foundation that your dream business will stand upon.

Questions To Ask Your Experts

Here are some questions to ask your expert council to create your own plan:

- What are going to be some of my startup expenses? How much should I expect to spend in inventory, equipment, marketing, etc, to get my business launched?
- How did you fund the start of your business?
- Are there financing options available to cover the startup costs?
- What were some of your biggest expenses?
- Did it cost more than expected? If so, how much?
- How much extra money should I set aside to help cover unexpected expenses?
- How long did it take you to get your business profitable?
- How long should I expect until I earn that money back?

Launch Date

The last thing you need to clarify is the launch date for your new business. Once you assemble your launch plan, think about how long it will take you to execute it. Give yourself some extra time. As I mentioned, things typically take longer than expected. If you think you can do it all in three months, it's probably best to give yourself six just to make sure you can do the job thoroughly.

Once you decide on a launch date, stick to it. Use it as a deadline to hold yourself accountable. Go through the entire Goal Crazy Cycle again with a focus on your business launch. Seek expert counsel to finish putting together your launch plan, set a Most Impactful Goal (ideally to launch your business, otherwise a target related to it), take messy action toward your goal, then reflect.

Here are some questions to ask your experts to make a plan for your launch date:

- How long did it take you to prepare for the launch of your business?
- How soon would you recommend me schedule my launch?
- When will I know I am ready to schedule my launch?
- What helped you get everything ready in time?
- How did you keep yourself organized?

Reflect And Implement

Fill out the Funding and Launch Date portions of your One-Page Launch Plan based on the exercises in this chapter. Make note of key questions you need help with so you can discuss the topics with your experts for guidance. Even if you think you know exactly how to do it all, still have an expert review your plan to make sure.

After you make your plan, use the Goal Crazy Cycle to execute it!

If you need help keeping yourself organized to get your business launched, check out our Goal Crazy Planner. It is designed for this! Plus, we have coaching programs where you can get personalized guidance. Check it all out at: GoalCrazy.com

PART 4

GROW AND SUSTAIN

CHAPTER 21

AFTER YOU START YOUR BUSINESS

In this chapter, I want to focus on what you will do *after* you get your business launched. If you follow the process and push through the challenges, you can make it here! But then what? What do you do next?

After I successfully launched Goal Crazy, I met with one of my coaches and told him how I accomplished my goal of starting an ecommerce business and I wasn't sure what to do next.

He said, "Jason, you climbed your first mountain. Now you need to look for the next one." He got a pen and paper and drew a simple image that explained it all.

He drew a stick figure at the bottom of a mountain. He said, "When you were standing at the bottom all you could see was the top of the mountain to climb.

But now you are at the top of this mountain! Now you can see there is another mountain, a bigger one behind it! However, to climb the next mountain, you need to go back down a portion of the mountain you just climbed in order to start up the next one. There will be a risk. There is always a learning curve."

He asked me, "What is the next mountain you can see now that you are at the top of this one?"

I said, "Well I want to start selling internationally. It seems like I can scale the exact process I am doing in other countries. But it will require me to invest in starting the processes over again there. I will need to invest in inventory, setting up distribution, and marketing to get my product known."

"It sounds like you have found your second mountain then!" he replied.

He then drew several more mountains after the second. The mountain range looked like a stock chart that was rising. The line would go up, then down roughly 30 percent, then rise up again higher than the prior peak. It went on and on until he drew it off the page.

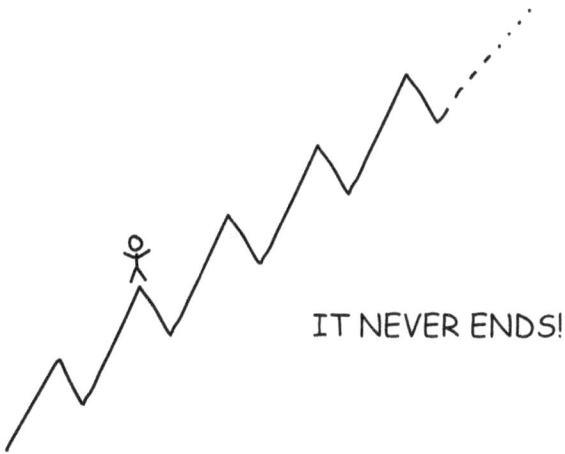

IT NEVER ENDS!

He said, "Here's the thing, this mountain range will go on forever, but right now the next mountain is blocking your view of the rest. You need to climb the second mountain, and then the third will be in sight. When you climb the third mountain, you will see the fourth. And so it will continue, you will start to see and climb each mountain one at a time."

This was a simple little image, but has been so true in my life! Here is what my mountain range has looked like for Goal Crazy.

- 1st Mountain: Launch planners in the USA.
- 2nd Mountain: Expand the business internationally
- 3rd Mountain: Start coaching
- 4th Mountain: Start a podcast
- 5th Mountain: Write a book.

There will be a mountain range of opportunities behind your business launch too. Once you get your business running, you will start to see new opportunities that you weren't even aware of before. The more actions you take, the more opportunities present themselves.

Let's say you start a simple carpet scrubbing business. After getting your business running and consistent, you notice many customers start asking if you can clean their furnace air ducts as well. You do some research and decide to launch another division in your business cleaning air ducts.

It takes an investment into the new equipment but it is much easier to launch this time because you already have a steady flow of customers that you can now upsell your new service to. It grows so much you hire employees and have multiple vans driving around servicing houses. One of your customers asks if you can clean the carpet at his business too. Then you realize an opportunity in the marketplace, start marketing your services to businesses, and launch a commercial division. It takes yet another investment into hiring more people and buying more equipment, but it's much easier because you have experience with these services now. You now have a large scale operation with dozens of employees, multiple crews, and several divisions that all started with a simple business cleaning carpet.

This is just an example, but I can't tell you how many times I have seen people's businesses start to grow and develop once they get started. I call this concept, Dream big, Do bigger!

Dream Big, Do Bigger

Once you start your business you will realize it is even better than you expected. Getting your business launched isn't an end in itself but the starting point of an entirely new type of life. It will be hard to see that when you are just getting started on the journey, but once you have the business, you will realize many more mountains are now in your view.

Oftentimes, we have the illusion that successful entrepreneurs had their entire business vision figured out before they started. In reality, they likely only saw the first mountain, then the second, third, and fourth mountains presented themselves after they started taking action.

Work hard to get this business started, and be prepared to see even better opportunities following it.

How To Grow Your Business

Let me give you a little advice on how to find these next mountains for your business. After you get it launched, there are two more "phases" that you will work through. The first is to stabilize your business, and the second is to scale it. Let me explain what I mean by each of these and how you can use the same Goal Crazy Cycle to do them.

Systematize Your Business

The launch of your business will be a very exciting time. You'll have big spikes in sales when marketing works, followed by stressful times when sales decline and you can't figure out why. That is why the next phase of your entrepreneurial journey is to stabilize and systematize your business so you can get consistent results.

To do this, we first need to remind ourselves of the dream lifestyle we want to create. Back in Chapter Six you wrote down a vision of the type of life you want to create. Look back at the lifestyle and work to determine how much money you need to make each month to support it. We will call this number your Freedom Factor. It represents the monthly income your business needs to earn to provide you the freedom to live your ideal lifestyle.

Often when I ask entrepreneurs what this freedom factor would be they just shout out random numbers like $20k per month. Rather than making a guess, I want you to actually calculate how much you need. Typically, entrepreneurs will realize they don't need as much as they expected.

What would your Freedom Factor be?

Once you determine it, you will need to establish three core processes to make this target consistently attainable. You'll need a consistent process for marketing, sales, and fulfillment. Below, I'll provide a short self assessment you can use to determine where you need to focus your efforts to make your Freedom Factor possible.

Marketing:
- Do you have a process to market your business that brings you consistent leads?
- Do these marketing efforts provide enough leads to make your income target possible?

Sales:

- Do you have a process to consistently generate sales from your leads?
- Are you selling at price points profitable enough to lead to your income target?

Fulfillment:

- Do you have a consistent process to fulfill all of the sales you obtain?
- Are you able to fulfill the sales volume needed to reach your income target?

These are the core processes to establish for you to hit your Freedom Factor. Obviously there are many other processes to form within each of these categories such as processes for accounting, inventory management, new employee training, etc. However, sales will be the lifeblood of your business, so getting consistency there will be key.

After you use the self assessment above to find the weak point in your business, then you can use the Goal Crazy Cycle to fix it. For example, maybe you realize that your marketing and fulfillment are great but your sales process doesn't convert a high enough percentage of leads to meet your income goal. Then use sales as your focus for the Goal Crazy Cycle.

Go find experts who perform at the sales volume you aspire to reach. You will find that once you have a business it will be much easier to form contacts in your industry because you will have more credibility. Ask these experts how they convert their leads into sales. Based on the information they give you, form a 90-day goal. Maybe the goal is to implement a new sales approach, hire a new salesperson, recreate your sales page online, or something completely different. Then take messy action, and reflect on your progress until you hit the goal

Once you create a replicable process for each of the three areas in your business, it will provide the opportunity to either scale your business or sell it. Without processes though, it will be difficult to do either! It will be hard to sell your business if there are no systems in place to operate it without you. And, if there are not clear processes, it will be difficult to scale because scaling disorganization turns to chaos.

Scale Or Sell

Once you create your replicable process, now you have the lovely decision of whether you want to scale your business to the next level or sell it. If you truly did find a business that you are passionate about, then you will likely want to keep it for the long run. However, I have met entrepreneurs that simply love the process of starting and selling businesses. If that is you, selling might be the best route.

The steps for each will look very different, but the Goal Crazy Cycle will work for both. Find someone who has already either scaled or sold their business and ask them how they did it. Follow the rest of the process from there.

No matter how big you get, don't let your pride get in the way of asking for help. Once you think you "know it all," that's when bad decisions are made. Even if you think you know exactly what you are doing, double check it with someone who has done it successfully before. At this point you have invested too much into this business to let a small error throw things off track.

Celebrate

Don't try to tackle the next mountain just because it's presented itself. Remember to take time to celebrate and enjoy launching your company. That is a huge accomplishment! Obviously having a company you love is a reward in itself, but it is important to do something extra to reward yourself for all the hard work that you put into starting it.

I was reminded of the importance of this the other day when I was getting something from the cupboard and our two-year-old son asked for some rice chex cereal. I reached into the box and handed them down to him. He filled his hands with the chex, but before he ate a single one, what do you think he asked for? More! If you have a two year old, I am sure you have had a similar experience.

I was thinking, "Dude, you haven't even taken a bite yet! Just eat what I gave you, then I'll give you more." But then it hit me—how often do I do the same thing and act with this two-year-old behavior? How often have I accomplished a goal of mine and before even taking one day to celebrate and relax, I think, "I need to accomplish another goal. I need *more*!"

Don't fall into this trap.

Clarify now how you will reward yourself once you hit your goal. Maybe there is something you want to buy, a trip you want to go on, a restaurant you want to eat at, or some other special way you want to celebrate. Don't be so focused on the next goal that you never take time to enjoy and appreciate the life you have created.

As part of my reflection process, I find accomplishments to celebrate. When I bought my very first rental property, I went and got myself a blazer jacket that I had really wanted. Even though I have had the jacket now for years, every time I wear it I am still reminded of how I bought my first rental property.

I like to regularly reward myself for smaller goals and milestones too. Sometimes when I hit small milestones I'll buy a fancy gel pen. They are only a few dollars so they don't cost much, but every time I use them, I'm reminded that I am an accomplisher. I try to surround myself with many of these little rewards as symbols to remind me that I can accomplish the goals I set for myself.

Treating yourself to these rewards also helps to combat burnout. It might seem silly but if you don't do this you will eventually feel like a machine that is always working on your business and never taking a break to enjoy the fruits of your labor. Find a way to celebrate!

Reflect And Implement

What are some of the mountains you have climbed? What is the mountain you are currently on?

_____

_____

_____

_____

What is the next mountain that is presenting itself? Is it worth the risk to start climbing it?

_____

_____

_____

_____

Have you taken time to celebrate your previous accomplishments? If not, how will you celebrate hitting your goal?

_____

_____

_____

_____

Download the My Mountains PDF exercise free at **GoalCrazy.com/ freedownloads** or by scanning the QR code below:

CHAPTER 22

AVOID BURNOUT

I want to help you avoid a common pitfall many entrepreneurs fall into that takes all the fun out of entrepreneurship.

Burnout.

Burnout has become increasingly well-recognized in our society, especially with entrepreneurs, because there is so little separation between their businesses and themselves. It's easy to fall into the trap of working on your business 24/7 and never having time to enjoy life.

I work with dozens of entrepreneurs who have become slaves to the very business they started to give them freedom. It's ironic, I know! They spend years with their head down working *in* their business and never stop to look up and work *on* their business. They work 80+ hours a week, never take days off, and barely earn enough money to pay their bills. This is the exact recipe for burnout. They will keep pushing along until eventually the stress of it all leads them to give up. I don't want this for you!

I often ask my clients, "Is your mind truly available to you?" If your mind is constantly worrying, trying to solve problems, and stressing about tasks, then it is not available to you. It's occupied. It's buried in the weeds of business and it will just be a matter of time before you hate the very business you started.

Luckily, there is an easy practice to implement that can save you from this struggle—taking regular time for silence. I know this sounds backward, maybe even too simple to work, but let me explain how silence helps and why this is a *must* for you as an entrepreneur.

To help you understand this, I want to tell you about an experience I had recently. After moving into our new house, we went through a phase of decorating and hanging many pictures on the walls. Often, when I was hanging a photo, I would have my wife come hold the frame so I could take a step back and look at it from a distance. By taking a step back, I could better see if the picture was straight and in the right spot on the wall. It was difficult to see the bigger perspective when I was only two inches away from the wall.

This is what happens in business too! We get so caught up in the mix of work that it is difficult to see the bigger picture. People get lost in the details of their business that they never stop to look up and see where they are headed.

This is where coaches often help. They are a few steps back away from all the action and can have a better view of what is happening. They can guide you. Luckily though, you can do this for yourself too even without a coach.

In order to do this for yourself, you need to take time for silence. You need to have empty time to take a step back from your business and look at it with a bigger perspective. I take time daily to sit in silence, journal out my thoughts, prayers, ideas, worries, and troubles.

Taking time for silence will result in two things: Clarity and energy.

People tell me all the time that they need more, "motivation." The word "motivation" is defined as "the process that initiates, guides, and maintains goal-oriented behaviors." The interesting thing is that silence will provide all these same things! Silence will provide you with the clarity to guide and maintain goal-oriented behaviors, and it will give you the energy to initiate it. When people tell me they need more motivation, typically what they need is more silence!

Clarity

Most people avoid being alone with their thoughts at all costs, then they are unsure why they don't understand themselves. What if you treated a friend this same way you treat yourself?

What if a friend invited you over because they were going through a really tough time and needed your help. Then, when your friend started to explain their troubles, you pulled out your phone and started scrolling social media while playing a podcast in the background. Would your friend feel important? Would they feel listened to? Of course not! Then why do we do this to ourselves?

When we have a free minute to be with ourselves and our thoughts we immediately pull out the phone and distract ourselves. No wonder we are confused and stressed! We don't give ourselves the space to process anything.

One of my favorite quotes is, "All of humanity's problems stem from man's inability to sit quietly in a room alone" by Blaise Pascal. I have found this quote to be so true. As I've made a commitment to taking regular time for silence in my life, I find the answers to my problems. Even more importantly, I often find that I have far fewer problems than I actually thought.

If you're new to the practice of taking time for silence, I think daily journaling is a really good place to start. When I get up each morning, before I look at my phone, eat, or do anything, I sit for one hour of silence to pray, journal, and reflect. I like to do this before my dreaming time, so I can empty my mind of all the stresses and worries that would otherwise distract my thoughts from my dreams.

This may sound unrealistic. That's okay, I will give you a strategy later in the chapter to help with this. If all you can commit to right now is just ten minutes, that is great. Sit down with a journal and start putting your thoughts on paper. Clear your mind so that you mentally take a step back from the busyness of your life and look at the bigger picture.

- Ask yourself:
    - What feels heavy right now?
    - What thoughts keep running through my mind?
    - Where am I comparing myself?
    - What do I wish I could be doing?
    - What would be fun to do?
    - What do I need to let happen?

You can download a free list of additional journaling prompts at GoalCrazy.com/freedownloads.

Energy

Another by-product of silence is energy. Even if you are working on your dreams and making lots of progress, you will still burn out if you never take a break. Burnout will lead to giving up!

Being busy taking action is a good thing, but too much work can be unhealthy. Busyness can become an addiction, and most of our society is indeed addicted to it. Obviously we need time to rest, and when we are well rested we have more energy. We all know this, but it's crazy how few people actually act on it. People brag about no days off and how busy their lifestyle is. To me that seems horrible!

Being "busy" has become a conditioned response to, "How are you?"

Look, having a full life is great, but if you are exhausted with no time left to enjoy your life, it's not worth it! Do you really want to be so attached to your business that you don't have time to enjoy the fruit of your labor? Didn't you start your business because you wanted freedom?

You may remember learning in school that even dirt in a field needs to rest every several years. If you never let it rest, you will strip the field of its nutrients and nothing new can grow. The same will happen to you if you never take a break. You will fry your mind and body.

I think of silence like the lever in a pinball machine. In order to start the game you pull the lever back to compress a spring. When you release the lever, the spring is released and launches the pinball forward to start the game. Silence does the same thing! If I don't take time for silence, the lever is never pulled back and you are left trying to thrust yourself into life. However, if you take silence, the spring is wound up, and when you return back to work, you are full of energy and launched into action.

Ultimately, it is up to you to determine if you are *too* busy or not. The main thing I want you to know is that if you do not create boundaries for your business, your work will almost always overtake your life. From the very beginning you need to *force* yourself to take time off.

Force The Time

What if taking ten minutes of silence each day could revolutionize your productivity? How often do you feel exhausted, stressed, or overwhelmed? When you feel that way, what are some things you do to numb that feeling away?

Maybe you scroll on social media, watch TV, read the news, or go drinking with friends. All of these are methods to *numb* the discomfort of feeling overwhelmed. They are forms of escapism. They distract you from dealing with your internal issues but don't solve them. They seem to fix the issue while you are engaging in them, but once you stop, the issues are right there again.

Taking time for silence will be more restful than these numbing activities. Rather than scrolling social media, what if you took 15 minutes to journal? Rather than watching a show, you could go on a walk through your neighborhood. These might seem like small changes, but they can lead to massive results. When you take genuine time for silence, you come back with clarity and energy. When you take time to binge watch TV, it leaves you feeling drained and still stressed about your challenges.

People often share with me that they get their best ideas in the shower. My first thought when I hear this is "Yeah, that's because it's probably the only time you have silence!" What if you could get that level of clarity and peace multiple times throughout the day?

So, how do you fit this in? First we need to recognize the "numbing" activities that you are currently doing and minimize or eradicate them.

Secondly, we need to force silence into your schedule. Yes, it needs to be forced in. It should not be something that fits in "if there is time." This needs to be a priority. Just like if your best friend was going through a hard time you would likely be willing to find ten minutes to talk with them throughout the day. Do the same for yourself. You are in the middle of starting a business, you are worth the ten minutes to simply be with yourself.

The best way to make this happen is to find a space where you can be free from distractions to make the silence happen. I like to sit in our guest bedroom or go on a walk in the park near our house. I need to separate myself from my phone, other people, and items that will remind me of work.

During this time of silence, sit and journal. Sit and be with yourself. Notice what you are feeling, what you are worried about, what you are excited about. You can access a collection of journal prompts, as well as guided meditations to do during this silent time on our website at **GoalCrazy. com/freedownloads**.

Put this in your calendar now. Find a ten minute block of time in the coming 24 hours to sit down without your phone, to be in silence.

Silence Gets Easier

When you first start taking time for silence, you might find that it takes effort. You will probably have an inner battle as you tell yourself to be silent, but your thoughts are racing with tasks that need your attention. At first silence may not feel comfortable or even relaxing. This is because your mind works like a fan. When you turn it off, it doesn't just stop. It spins slower and slower until it eventually comes to rest. Your mind will do the same. The more silent time you take, the more the internal fan will slow down.

If you are new to this habit, it will require effort. You will be developing the discipline to sit and be with yourself rather than the habitual skill of distracting yourself. Like any new skill, it will be awkward at first. But the longer you do it, the easier it will get. The more your internal fan will begin to slow down and bring you peace. The key will be making a commitment to doing this daily. If you do, you will realize you have all the motivation already within you once you let your mind find a level of peace.

Mindset Day

The other strategy that will prevent burnout is to schedule days off. As crazy as it sounds I work with many entrepreneurs that never take days off. Even on the days they consider to be their "off days" they respond to emails, run errands, and do paper work at home.

You *need* days off! If you don't get in the habit right away of taking them, you will find that work fills your entire life. To help my clients with this, we developed the concept of the Mindset Day. A Mindset Day is a complete day off. No phone calls, no emails, no paperwork, just time to relax. I call it a "mindset" day because this is one of the highest payoff things you can do for your mindset. And, as you know, your mindset plays a *huge* role in your success. Taking time off *is* a productive activity.

Once a quarter I block off an entire work day for my mindset. During this day, I take time for silence, reflection and fun. A Mindset Day has two primary components: time for silence and time to have fun.

On a Mindset Day, I don't do any work at all. No emails, no calls, no meetings. If possible I don't even carry my phone. I get up, have a slow morning and just enjoy life. I spend the morning in prayer and silence to clear my head of thoughts and worries. I might do light reading or goal setting activities to bring inspiration. I don't try to solve my problems, instead the focus is to get myself to relax.

In the afternoon, I do something that I enjoy. For example, I may go for a walk at the park, a bike ride, hot tubbing, or visit family. I just enjoy life.

How often do you schedule time to simply relax and enjoy life? For most people, the answer is "never." That's what a Mindset Day is for—to force yourself to stop working and enjoy life.

It is after or during a Mindset Day I get my best ideas. I get to step outside of my normal routine, get outside of the challenges of my life, and be at peace. I am reminded of the beautiful world we have and all the opportunities in it.

Now, many of my clients feel guilty doing this at first. Maybe you can relate. They feel like they must always be productive and don't deserve to have one day for themselves. I immediately tell them, "No wonder you're feeling burnout and overwhelmed with life. You've been so busy you've forgotten what it feels like to actually live. Go relax and enjoy yourself!"

I will warn you, the first time you do this you will have thoughts that tell you it is a waste of time, lazy, or that you weren't actually tired in the first place. Don't listen to them. You need this, you are worth the time. You will burn yourself out if you don't have this.

Once you try this, you will quickly realize the power of it. If you want energy and clarity (a.k.a motivation), a Mindset Day is a must.

It's vital during this day to spend time with truly energizing activities. Don't spend the day drinking, playing video games, or watching movies. These numb you to life rather than helping you experience it.

Look in your calendar for the next 30 days and schedule your first Mindset Day. Put it in your calendar. Aim to get in at least one Mindset Day per quarter. As you get your business more streamlined, try and make this once a month or week.

Reflect And Implement

When will you take time each day for silence? Morning? Afternoon? Evening? Put it in your calendar and set an alert in your phone now to remind you to take this time.

_____

_____

_____

_____

When will your Mindset Day be? Look at your calendar and block this day off. If you need to call off work, do it.

_____

_____

_____

_____

You can download our free Impactful Silence kit at **GoalCrazy.com/ freedownloads** and access journaling prompts, meditations, and helpful exercises to do during your time of silence. Or, scan the QR code below:

CHAPTER 23

CONCLUSION

Throughout this book I've been talking about how rewarding it is to start your dream business. I want to let you in on a little secret. Forming your dream business is great; but there is something even more fulfilling, and that's when your dream business forms *you*!

The years I worked on creating my business have formed me into a completely different person. A better person! And this has been a bigger reward than any of my accomplishments.

I don't think I realized this until the night before I proposed to my wife. There were a lot of thoughts that went through your mind before an event like this. I kept asking myself, "How did I end up with such a great woman?"

It was somewhere in that process I realized the power of my dreams. I realized how much the struggles, problems, and successes of my business had formed me. Several years prior, I was an immature, reckless kid, and somehow over the course of a few short years I completely changed.

For the first time ever, I started to feel grateful for the challenges I had received. When I originally started Goal Crazy, I literally thought I would launch the planner and become rich overnight. I thought I would be earning thousands of dollars per month passively and have the freedom to go do whatever I wanted. Luckily, my business took longer to succeed. It was hard! It challenged me entirely. It challenged me so much that I needed to remove bad habits, change friend groups, and live a healthier lifestyle. It challenged me to start analyzing the fears and limiting beliefs that had held me back in the past and to find ways to work through them. Somehow it even shifted my faith to be at the center of my life.

I'm sharing because I want you to know that your dreams have the potential to form you too. Your business can form you into a more disciplined, hardworking, courageous person.

One of the themes I've noticed as I talk to entrepreneurs on my podcast, is that entrepreneurship is ultimately a journey inside of yourself. It's a journey of self discovery as you uncover your true desires and push past the limiting beliefs you have about yourself.

When I started the journey toward my dreams, one of my dominating thoughts was, "What do I want to do with my life?" As I started getting clarity on that question, slowly my thoughts went deeper. I asked myself, "Who am I?" I began to see that all my life I had been trying to answer this one question. I had been trying to understand who I was, reveal who I was, improve who I was, or even prove who I was. I had just never realized it before.

This will also be the case for you. A business will start out as an external journey toward a goal, but turn into an internal journey to better understand yourself. I hope you can make it through both of these levels because it adds so much more meaning and purpose to your life.

Generational Change

Starting your dream business won't just change your life, it will change the lives of everyone around you. I have had many people tell me that seeing me follow my dreams has given them the confidence to follow theirs. Yours will do the same! Additionally it has the potential to change people's lives for generations to come. This isn't just about changing your life, this is about changing your kids, grandkids, and great grandkids lives too.

One of the main reasons I have been able to follow my dreams is because of a man named Rudy. Rudy passed away before I was born, but still his influence has altered my life.

Rudy's family didn't have much. To make things worse, his mother passed away when he was just 12 years old, so Rudy dropped out of school in the sixth grade to help out around their family farm.

Around the age of 15, he decided he wanted more for his life and moved away from home. Even though he was a kid with only a sixth grade education and a small likelihood of success, he decided to take 100 percent accountability for the direction of his life and work to create a better future for himself.

He hitchhiked to another city, snuck into a farmer's barn, and slept in the hay bales. He couldn't get a job because he was only a kid. So, he walked up to a random construction site and just started working. After about a week, the job site manager realized he wasn't an employee and was furious. But because of Rudy's unbelievable work ethic and determination, the manager hired him on the spot.

Rudy had a bigger dream though—to become a pilot. He worked every single day for over two years at his construction job, including holidays and during horrific storms. Eventually he saved up money to enroll in a flight training school and become a pilot. He saved up more money, purchased his own plane, and started a small charter business flying wealthy individuals around.

Rudy kept dreaming bigger. He bought his own airport, started multiple flight training schools, and was eventually asked to build a flight school to train thousands of US Air Force pilots.

Later in life, he decided to get out of the airplane business and purchased car dealerships. Those car dealerships were passed down to my grandpa, then my father and uncle, and will eventually get passed on to my cousins and possibly siblings.

You see, Rudy was my great grandfather, and his courage to pursue his dream, despite the many struggles he faced, has changed the direction of our family's life for generations.

This is not because he went out and earned a bunch of money. Oftentimes people have this concept that generational wealth is the end goal. Generational wealth may be helpful, but what is even more powerful are generational habits. My great grandpa formed habits that have been passed down to us. He formed habitual ways of thinking, working, leading, and viewing life. These habits have allowed our family to succeed. It is because of those habits that were passed down to me that I am where I am in my life.

Rudy had every reason to feel like a victim. He was dealt a rough hand in life and could have easily given up on his dreams and himself. He could have easily found a reason to complain about his upbringing, about not having an education, not having a wealthy family or college degree. But he didn't. He proved to us that success doesn't come from a privileged background, but from the courage to work hard toward your dreams.

Although I never had the chance to meet Rudy, it is because he allowed his dreams to form him and change the direction of his life that I have the life I have now.

You have this same opportunity! You can change your life, and the lives of generations to come. What if you create the generational habit of taking 100 percent accountability for your life, your dreams, and your circumstances? Rather than finding reasons to be a victim, find ways to be a success. How could this business impact the future of your family's life?

If you have bad generational habits or circumstances passed down to you, I'm sorry, I know life often isn't fair. But, regardless of your situation, whether it is beautiful or ugly, you can decide where you want to go from here. You can become a victim or you can be a victor. You can be like Rudy, and change the direction of your family's legacy for generations to come.

The world needs your business! There are people who need you and your business's help. By following your dreams, you aren't just helping yourself. You are providing a service to our world and the future of humanity. Our society is driven forward by action-taking dreamers like yourself.

Now get out there and get your dream business started!

Reflect And Implement

I am on a mission to help aspiring entrepreneurs clarify their dream business and get it started.

If you know someone else who needs help starting a business, please recommend this book to them. Give them a copy or share with them some of the free resources, videos, or podcast episodes we have available at our website.

Additionally, if you need help implementing what you have learned in this book, we can help you! Schedule a free consultation with us at **GoalCrazy.com/freecall**

If you haven't accessed all your free bonuses that accompany this book, go check them out at **GoalCrazy.com/freedownloads** or scan the QR code below:

WANT TO FAST-TRACK YOUR BUSINESS LAUNCH?

At GoalCrazy.com, we offer programs designed to help you launch your dream business—no matter where you are on your entrepreneurial journey. Whether you need help clarifying your business idea, creating a launch plan, improving your mindset, managing your time, or simply staying accountable, we've got you covered. Our programs and supportive community are here to guide you every step of the way.

And be sure to check out the Goal Crazy Planner to help you make these principles part of your daily life.

Learn more at GoalCrazy.com

URGENT PLEA!

Thank You For Reading My Book!

I really appreciate all of your feedback and I love hearing
what you have to say. I need your input to make the next
version of this book (and my future books) better.

Please take two minutes now to leave a helpful review on
Amazon letting me know what you thought of the book.

GoalCrazy.com/review

Thanks so much!

Jason VanDevere

ABOUT THE AUTHOR

JASON VANDEVERE is an entrepreneur and the founder of Goal Crazy Ltd., which offers courses, coaching, and programs to help aspiring entrepreneurs start their dream business. After leaving his family's successful car dealership business, Jason built a multi-million dollar real estate portfolio and created the best-selling *Goal Crazy Planner*, used by tens of thousands to set and achieve personal and professional goals. He's been featured in *Fast Company*, *Money.com*, and *Markets Insider* and today he shares his insights as a speaker and host of the *Goal Crazy Podcast*. Jason lives with his wife and three children. He's passionate about inspiring others to pursue their dreams—even the crazy ones!

BIBLIOGRAPHY

Chapter 6:

Disney, Walt, producer. *Alice in Wonderland*. Directed by Clyde Geronimi, Wilfred Jackson, and Hamilton Luske. Burbank, CA: Walt Disney Productions, 1951.

Chapter 11:

Fryar CD, Carroll MD, Afful J. "Prevalence of overweight, obesity, and severe obesity among adults aged 20 and over: United States, 1960–1962 through 2017–2018." NCHS Health E-Stats, CDC, Revised January 29, 2021. https://www.cdc.gov/nchs/data/hestat/obesity-adult-17-18/obesity-adult.htm#Citation

Chapter 12:

Keller, Gary, and Jay Papasan. *The ONE Thing: The Surprisingly Simple Truth Behind Extraordinary Results*. Austin, TX: Bard Press, 2013.

Chapter 14:

McKay, Brett. Interview (#947: Turn Your Anxiety Into a Strength) with Dr. David Rosmarin. *The Art of Manliness Podcast*. Podcast Audio. November 29, 2023. **https://www.artofmanliness.com/health-fitness/health/podcast-947-turn-your-anxiety-into-a-strength/**

Dematte, Dan. Bream Bigger. 1st Edition. Manchester, NH. Sophia Institute Press, 2021.

Chapter 22:

Cherry, Kendra. "Motivation: The Driving Force Behind Our Actions." *Verywell Mind*, Dotdash Media, last modified May 3, 2023. **https://www.verywellmind.com/what-is-motivation-2795378**.

.

.

www.ingramcontent.com/pod-product-compliance
Lightning Source LLC
Chambersburg PA
CBHW071550210326
41597CB00019B/3185